LIVING WITH GOD'S KIDS

ALSO BY KAY KUZMA

Building Character (Coauthored with Jan Kuzma)
Child Study Through Observation and Participation
Don't Step on the Pansies
Guidelines for Child Care Centers
My Unforgettable Parents
Nursery School and Day Care Center Management Guide (Coauthored with Clare Cherry and Barbara Harkness)
Teaching Your Own Preschool Children
The Kim, Kari and Kevin Storybook
Understanding Children
Understanding Children Study Guide
Working Mothers (Previously titled *Prime-Time Parenting*)
Filling Your Love Cup

Living with GOD'S KIDS

Today's guide for Christian parents, grandparents and anyone else who has the privilege and responsibility of living with one of God's special children.

KAY KUZMA, Ed.D.

Published by

Box 2222
Redlands, California 92373 USA

Printed by
THE QUIET HOUR
Redlands, California 92373 USA

Scripture quotations, unless otherwise noted, are from the King James version of the Bible.

Special permission has been granted for sections of the book which were previously published as articles.

"The Ladder of Life," *Life and Health,* December 1977, and "Make Your Family a Winning Team," *These Times,* September 1981 (Washington D.C.: Review and Hearld Publishing Association).

"Turning the 'Terrible' Into the 'Terrific,'" Winter 1982, and "Learning to Love and Respect Authority," Fall 1981, *Focus* (Washington D.C.: General Conference of Seventh-day Adventists).

"The Working Mother's Challenge," *College People,* February 1983 (Lincoln, Nebraska: Union College).

The Voice of Prophecy has granted permission for the use of radio spot material written by Kay Kuzma.

Library of Congress Catalog Card Number: 83-61552

ISBN 0-910529-03-5

Manufactured in the United States of America

Dedicated to my mother,
IRENE G. HUMPAL
I'm proud to be her child as well as God's

CONTENTS

PREFACE

Every parent has been commissioned by God for a special work—the nurturing and molding of His little ones. The task is awesome; the responsibility great. Yet, seeing a child choose Christ's gift of salvation, knowing that your example and teaching influenced his or her decision, is a reward that has no equal.

Children are a gift to us from God. We should not treat them as our own—to do with them as our fancies, feelings, and frustrations dictate. We must love them, teach them and discipline them as Christ would.

Let's follow God's words of instruction. Let's make our homes little heavens on earth and thank the Lord daily for the privilege of living with His kids.

"Lo, children are a heritage of the Lord: and the fruit of the womb is his reward." Psalm 127:3.

How to Build Character In an Imperfect World

To attempt to build a child's character without a plan is as foolish as building a house without blueprints.

Second Peter 1:5-7 is God's step-by-step plan for the character development of His children. ". . . add to your faith virtue; and to virtue knowledge; And to knowledge temperance (self-control); and to temperance patience (endurance); and to patience godliness; And to godliness brotherly kindness; and to brotherly kindness charity (love)."

It is interesting how often preparation for the labor of childbirth receives more attention than preparation for the labor of child rearing. And yet it is the labor of child rearing that has the lasting effect.

Sixteen-year-old Gerald Evans was stumbling on his ladder of life. Picked up for reckless driving and possession of marijuana, he had gotten himself even deeper in trouble by impulsively taking a swing at one of the arresting officers.

His parents were again waiting for their son, this time to be delivered to them by a police officer. But this delivery was even harder than the one sixteen years ago, for at birth their hopes and dreams for their sons's highest potential knew no limits. And now, after sixteen years, he was unhappy, rebellious, failing in school, and in trouble with the law. Where had they failed? They both worked hard trying to give Gerald every advantage—wholesome food, clothing, good schools.

They knew all the theories of child development. They knew that no matter where a child is born, no matter who his parents are, each will grow and develop in orderly sequence. All over the world babies sit before they crawl, crawl before they walk, and begin talking at approximately the same time. This is true even for babies who are swaddled for a good share of their first year.

Psychologists have tried to organize a child's development into different stages. Freud theorized psycho-sexual stages, while Piaget talks about cognitive stages; and Erik Erikson developed a psycho-social theory of development where he created eight stages through which man advances (see chart). And yet with all this knowledge, something was missing.

I believe this missing link can be found in the Bible in 2 Peter 1:5-7 where Peter wrote, "Giving all diligence, add to your faith virtue; and to virtue knowledge; and to knowledge temperance; and to temperance patience; and to patience godliness; and to godliness brotherly kindness; and to brotherly kindness charity." Each step is based upon achieving the previous step. This theory of development is a life ladder for each child who advances on it. It is the ladder of character development and could be termed the psycho-spiritual theory of development. Even though Peter gives no indication when these significant steps should be established in a person's life, it is not unreasonable to correlate them with Erikson's eight stages of man.

COMPARISON OF PSYCHO-SOCIAL AND PSYCHO-SPIRITUAL STAGES OF DEVELOPMENT

Stage	Erik Erickson's Psycho-social stages	Peter's Psycho-spiritual stages
1. Birth-1	Trust	Faith
2. 1-3	Autonomy	Virtue
3. 4-5	Initiative	Knowledge
4. 6-11 (school age)	Industry	Temperance
5. 11-19 (adolescence)	Identity	Patience
6. Young adult (dating and marriage)	Intimacy	Godliness
7. Adulthood (parental)	Generativity	Brotherly kindness
8. Maturity	Integrity and self-acceptance	Love/Charity

Keith and Mary Evans' knowledge of psychological theories of child development gave them a good insight into the stages children would go through as they develop. They knew from Erikson's eight stages of man, for example, that they should expect Gerald to be autonomous at 2 and 3 years of age. He had no difficulty being autonomous—he wanted his own way and got it. The problem was that the theories only told his parents what to expect, and not what to teach.

The idea that children should be left alone to develop in their own way is wrong. Children are like roses; they must have a good environment, water, sun, and good earth, but this alone won't produce the loveliest blossoms. Roses must be carefully pruned at the right time and place and consistently trained to grow in their proper place amid all the other flowers of the garden—or they grow wild. If children aren't lovingly pruned and consistently trained they too will grow wild. Just as it takes laboring to produce roses, it takes a lot to produce beautiful children.

What Keith and Mary Evans needed was a practical guide of what to teach Gerald while he was young.

Peter's ladder of life has steps that can contribute to the development of children with beautiful characters.

Step 1—Faith. It must be established early in a child's life. The way a child is treated by his parents will primarily determine whether he can learn to trust them, as well as others. As the parents consistently meet the child's needs, he begins to realize that even though he may have to wait, his mother will eventually come and take care of him. Faith also means that he knows enough about his parents to accept them as authorities. When this foundation has been laid, the child is ready for the next step.

Step 2—Virtue. Honesty, purity, and integrity are only a few of the virtues a young child must begin learning so he can function in a family or society without exhibiting disruptive and unacceptable behavior. A child learns through his mistakes that some types of behavior are punished. He also learns that other behavior makes his parents pleased. Even though living virtuously takes a lifetime, the roots of right and wrong are established during a child's first three years.

Step 3—Knowledge. Even though a child begins learning from birth, it almost seems that his thirst for knowledge increases when he starts asking, "Why?" It is during these preschool years that children actively seek and experiment in order to find answers, instead of simply absorbing the information given by others. Clues about what types of learning opportunities should be provided to children should come directly from the child himself, rather than from relying on what adults think children should learn.

If you were asked, "What knowledge should parents teach children?" you would probably reply, as the majority of adults do, "The alphabet and how to count." In reality these things hold very little meaning for children, and the only delight in mastering them is the pleasure it gives their parents. What preschoolers really want to know is "Why is the sky blue?" "Why can't I touch the rainbow?" "Why does heat make some things harder, like pudding, and other things softer, like margarine?"

Step 4—Temperance. Temperance is based on knowledge. If a child doesn't know that sugar is bad for his teeth and health, he will usually choose the sweetest food (cake, ice cream, et cetera) when given a choice between dessert and a vegetable or entree. After he knows what is good for him, he can then begin mastering the self-control necessary to follow what he knows.

Step 5—Patience. Young children seem to be naturally impatient, but I have often wondered whether it is because they are born that way or because adults are so often impatient with them. True, patience can come only after a child has been able to exhibit self-control, which is part of temperance. Patience is acquired through patience. A parent can help a child to be more patient by not making unreasonable demands on him, by standing close to a child when patience is required, and by lending the child support and encouragement. A parent must also be careful not to reward a child's impatient demands by giving in to them.

Step 6—Godliness. True godliness can come only after a child's faith has been established, he knows right from wrong, he knows what is good for him, and has the self-control to keep away from the harmful and be willing to wait for those good things. Godliness is perhaps not fully established until after those self-centered adolescent years, when a person can finally look outside himself to others. This understanding of others can allow a person to exhibit more Christlike traits than was possible previously. The foundation for this trait lies in early childhood, when parents teach their children what God is like, and inspire in them a desire to be like Him.

Step 7—Brotherly kindness. Most parents would give almost anything if they could only teach their children a little of this virtue. Children seem to be so harsh with one another. "Shut up," "dumb, dumb," "stupid," words like these are only too familiar among young children. Kindness, thoughtfulness, politeness, are all important, but if a child doesn't learn these early, then he develops a life style of rudeness, injuring others, which is difficult to change as he gets older. An example of true brotherly kindness, where one is willing to give all for another, is found in parental love for children.

Step 8—Love/Charity. It is more than kindness—it is the love of man for his fellow man. True love comes by giving, not from receiving. The more you do for another person, even though he may not be attractive, the more you will grow to love him. Love is a principle, not a feeling. You can do something for unlovable people, and your love for them will grow. A young child's love is perhaps the purest and most uncomplicated, but it seems as though most of us lose this some time between early childhood and adulthood, only to regain it after years of maturity. Our task as parents is to keep this alive throughout childhood.

And so a child is born ready to advance on the life ladder, depending primarily on his parents to guide each step. What can a parent do to ensure a foundation for each rung of the ladder?

- Show your child you have faith—faith in God, in others, and in him.
- Live a virtuous life. Be careful about what you watch on television. Resist the temptation to tell that white lie or to remain silent when the clerk forgets to charge you for

something.

• Continue to seek after knowledge. Let your child see you spend some time at the library, let him see you read, and experiment as you solve problems.

• Be temperate. Avoid the afternoon snack or staying up late at night.

• Be patient even under the most trying circumstances.

• Respect God and live a godly life.

• Be the good Samaritan—take time to be thoughtful; show that you care.

• Show the child he is loved by spending time with him. Let him see you giving love to others by doing things for them.

How will your child progress on the ladder of life? Will he be like Gerald, who stumbled because of lack of clear guidelines, or will he develop the kind of character that will stand for right and good?

The labor involved in getting a child into the world must become a labor of love in helping the child to reach his full potential.

With God's plan you can build beautiful characters for Him in this imperfect world in which we live.

Lessons From Hannah, The Absent Mother

The Bible shares many examples of Godly parents, but one is especially striking. It's Hannah, because she spent so little time with Samuel and yet had such a tremendous impact.

Hannah only had three years to live with Samuel. By God's grace, parents today will have 12 to 18 years. But even if it's less, our influence can still be significant. The story of Hannah brings hope to thousands of "part-time" parents who by divorce or time-consuming traveling jobs are unable to spend the quantity of time they desire with their children.

How can we best use these precious years together so we can raise our children for God? Perhaps we can start by praying for our children and dedicating them to God's service, as did Hannah.

"For this child I prayed; and the Lord hath given me my petition which I asked of him: Therefore also I have lent him to the Lord; as long as he liveth he shall be lent to the Lord." 1 Samuel 1:27, 28.

One well-known inspirational writer mentions four

persons as examples of devoted and faithful mothers of all the women in the Bible. Hannah, the mother of Samuel, is mentioned along with Jochebed, who risked her life to save her son Moses' life, and then trained him for 12 years before he went to live in the palace of the Pharaoh; Elisabeth, John the Baptist's mother, who followed the strict instructions given to her by an angel as to how to rear her child; and Mary, Jesus' mother, who was given the honored task of bearing God's Son and after that, training Him for almost 26 years.[1]

It is easy to understand why Jochebed, Elisabeth, and Mary are listed, but why Hannah? She kept her son only long enough to wean him and then give him to Eli, the high priest, to raise.

What would you think of me if, when my little boy Kevin was 3 years old, I sent him to live with the president of the General Conference and went to see him only once a year when I brought him a new coat? I can hear you accusing me of child neglect or quoting to me some of the research findings by John Bowlby concerning the emotional reaction of anxiety and depressions that children have when they are deprived of their mother's and father's attention during the early years of life.[2]

But let's say I had a good motive. I didn't leave him because I wanted to run around and have a good time; I had promised the Lord that if He sent me a boy, I would dedicate him to the Lord's work, and placing Kevin in this man's care was the accepted way to be trained for the ministry. This sounds somewhat reasonable, but let us suppose that the president to whom I entrusted Kevin was as poor a father as was Eli. Eli's sons were corrupt. They made fun of the church services, stole offerings, and even forced the church members to give bigger offerings so they could take the best part for themselves.

This situation was so reprehensible that people had even stopped coming to church. Everyone knew that Eli was to blame, because he never wanted to cross his sons by disciplining them. What kind of father would a man such as this be for Kevin? What kind of influence would undisciplined sons have on him? You would probably think I was out of my mind to leave a little boy, just barely weaned from his bottle, in this kind of home.

But let's say Kevin grew up to be a strong church leader and eventually became president of the General Conference. What would you think of me as a mother? You would probably say, "Isn't it amazing what Kevin became in spite of his mother's lack of influence in his life after he was 3?"

Yet Hannah, one of the examples given as a good mother, left her little boy Samuel, just barely weaned (probably about 3 years of age), with Eli, the high priest, amid the corruption and evil that Eli's two sons, Hophni and Phinehas, were bringing to the tabernacle service and the nation.

Why, then, did Samuel turn out so well?

A child needs at least three things in order to develop a healthy personality. These are love, discipline, and independence. The most important ingredient is love (affection and warmth) supplied to a child by his parents. It is impossible to give a child too much love as long as the child has adequate discipline, just enough to teach the child how to discipline himself, but not so much as to break his will. Finally, the child needs to be allowed to become increasingly independent as his ability to discipline himself increases.

Why did Samuel turn out so well? I think God worked through all three of the significant people in Samuel's life —Hannah, his mother; Elkanah, his father; and Eli, his foster parent—using each of their special characteristics to give Samuel the love, discipline, and independence he needed to become the spiritual leader of God's people.

Hannah's Influence

Hannah had high expectations for her firstborn son, the child for whom she had waited long. She knew that God had a special work for him. It is interesting that the mothers whom Ellen White mentions as good mothers (Hannah, Jochebed, Elisabeth, and Mary) had in common the knowledge that God had chosen their sons to do some great work. Could such a knowledge affect a mother's or parents' relationship to their children? Results of studies suggest that if parents or teachers have a high expectation for their children, such children are more likely to reach a high goal.

Such an effect was demonstrated recently in an experiment conducted in an elementary school. After the pupils were given an intelligence test, researchers selected at random five or six children in each class and told the teacher that these children, on the basis of the tests, were "spurters." At the end of the year all the children were retested. Those children who had been randomly selected and labeled as spurters made a significantly higher gain on the second intelligence test than did the other children in the class. The younger the children were, the more the effect of the teacher's expectation. For example, the average increase in IQ for the spurters in first grade was 27.4 points; in second grade it was only 16.5 points. By the fourth grade there was little effect.[3]

Hannah not only had high expectations for Samuel, she also knew that she had only a few short years to train him, since she had promised him to the Lord, and to fulfill this promise she must take him to Shiloh to live with Eli.

Three years is a short time, but the important consideration is that Hannah had Samuel for the first three years of his life, which are the most important years. A child learns more during these years than he will ever again learn. Benjamin Bloom, a noted psychologist, suggested, after reviewing more than 2,000 studies on children, that approximately 50 percent of a child's intellectual ability is acquired by 4 years of age; 80 percent by 8 years of age.[4] Research on disadvantaged children who are 3 and 4 years of age suggests that by this time it is too late to make a significant difference in their learning pattern, for this has already been established earlier in their lifetime.

The first three years are a time not only of fast mental growth but also of character development. Some have suggested that parents have three years to mold a child's will. If they haven't done it by that time, it will be hard to bring the child to submit to wholesome discipline.[5] It has also been said that after seven years of age, the character and personality have become stabilized, and it is only with tremendous effort that these characteristics can be changed later in life.[6]

Knowing she had only a few years to train Samuel before he went to live with Eli, who was such a poor father, I'm sure that Hannah spent every precious moment she could with her baby, preparing him for that situation. Hannah loved Samuel with all of the devotion of a mother's heart. And every day, as she watched him grow and listened to his childish gibberish, her affection entwined about him more closely. Can you imagine how hard it must have been for Hannah to give up this special God-given child? We often hear about the faith and courage of Abraham to sacrifice his only son, but I'm sure Hannah had this same faith and courage to give her son so early into God's service. In order to fit him for this service, she attempted to direct his thoughts to the Creator by every familiar object that surrounded him. She must have worked constantly in molding his character and will, because by the time he came to live with Eli he was kind, generous, obedient, and respectful. He was helpful and affectionate and beyond his age in spiritual maturity, so that while he was still a child the ephod was placed on him as a token of his consecration to the work of the sanctuary (the customary age for receiving the ephod was 25).

Hannah's influence on her son did not end when Samuel was brought to live in the sanctuary. Even though she was physically separated from him, he was constantly in her thoughts and prayers. Every year she made with her own hands a robe of service for him, and when she went up with her husband to worship at Shiloh, she gave this to Samuel as a reminder of her love. Ellen White says that every fiber of the little garment had been woven with a prayer that he might be pure, noble, and true. She did not ask God for Samuel to have worldly greatness, but she prayed earnestly that he might attain that greatness that Heaven values—that he might honor God and bless his fellow men. I'm sure that Samuel knew clearly how much his mother loved him and that she was praying for him daily. Hence, even though she was absent from Samuel for most of his life, her infuence remained strong.

"When Samuel shall receive the crown of glory, he will wave it in honor before the throne and gladly acknowledge that the faithful lessons of his mother, through the merits of Christ, have crowned him with immortal glory."[7]

It is important not to overlook Elkanah's influence upon Samuel. Elkanah, Samuel's father, was a man of wealth and influence, but he wasn't without faults. When he and Hannah had not had a child, the desire to pass on his name was so great that he took another wife at Hannah's insistence in order to have children. As years went by, the house became not only full of children but also full of jealousy and strife on the part of Peninnah, Elkanah's second wife. Peninnah was jealous and narrow-minded, proud and insolent. Hannah took all Peninnah's insults with meekness, but it caused her such agony that this conflict is what prompted her to plead with the Lord so fervently that when Eli saw her he thought she was drunk.

Elkanah had perhaps more influence on Samuel than we might realize. First of all, he was compassionate, kind, and loving, especially to Hannah. He deeply understood the hurt he had caused Hannah by marrying Peninnah, and tried to make it up even by going so far as giving childless Hannah a second portion of offering to give at the yearly sacred festivitics at Shiloh, while giving only one portion to Peninnah and each of her children. This only made Peninnah more jealous, and she taunted Hannah unmercifully about her childless state as evidence of the Lord's displeasure, until Hannah could stand it no longer.

Unable to hide her grief, she wept without restraint, and withdrew from the feast. Elkanah showed his love to her with these words in trying to comfort her, "Why weepest thou? and why eatest thou not? and why is thy heart grieved? am I not better to thee than ten sons?"[8] It's an old cliche, but it is also true: "The best gift a father can give to his children is to love their mother." I doubt whether Hannah could have been so successful with Samuel during those first three years if Elkanah had not been supportive of her efforts.

The first three years of a child's life are important for the child's healthy sexual identity. If a boy does not have a father image during this time, he will grow up to have more feminine characteristics than will other boys. But a father's influence upon his children is also strong in the areas of values and life styles.

For example, in a study completed on the student body at Pacific Union College, it was found that those students who came from homes where their father was the only vegetarian were more often vegetarians than were those who came from homes where the mother was the only vegetarian.[9]

In a youth study conducted by the Southeastern California Conference of Seventh-day Adventists, it was found that the children of an Adventist father and a non-Adventist mother were stronger Adventists and rated on the level of college students in their maturity of religious thought. On the other hand, their high school peers who came from homes where the mother was an Adventist and their father was not rated lower on both counts.[10] These findings seem to indicate that even though the father may not spend as much time with his children as a mother does, the influence of his life style upon his children is strong. It may well be that Samuel became the kind of person he was because of the strong, religiously dedicated, and devoted father he had.

Eli's Influence

What influence did Eli, who was such a poor father to his own sons, have upon Samuel? Unable to control them, he shrank from his duty of teaching them the right way of life. He was indulgent. He loved peace and ease. He did not exercise his authority to correct their evil habits and desires. Rather than contend with them and punish them, he submitted to their will and gave them their own way. Instead of regarding the education of his sons as one of the most important of his responsibilities, he treated the matter as of little consequence, and his sons grew up to be corrupt and evil men.

What if Samuel, at 3 years of age, had been a headstrong, disobedient, irreverent child? What if he had not been self-disciplined? What if he had had no respect for authority? Think what would have happened to 3-year-old Samuel living with Eli, who was loving and permissive and not willing to discipline him. It would have meant Samuel's downfall. As it turned out, Samuel had received his discipline from his mother and father. He knew how to obey. He had learned to be respectful, generous, and kind. So what this little 3-year-old boy really needed was someone who was warm, affectionate, and loving, and willing to allow him to grow in independence. I have a feeling that no father ever loved his child more tenderly than Eli loved Samuel.

In summary, a child needs love, discipline, and independence in order to develop a healthy personality, and Samuel received these from Hannah, Elkanah, and Eli. Hannah should be ranked high among mothers, for she did not have all the years that most of us have to influence our children. Through love and discipline, Hannah, with Elkanah's help, accomplished the molding of Samuel's character and personality in just three short years. Samuel was then ready for the finishing touches of love and independence that Eli was able to give him. "And the child Samuel grew on, and was in favour both with the Lord, and also with men."[11]

Finding Time to Parent

There is a time for everything, so the wise man said.

"A time to be born, and a time to die;

A time to plant, and a time to pluck up that which is planted;

A time to kill, and a time to heal;

A time to break down, and a time to build up;

A time to weep, and a time to laugh;

A time to mourn, and a time to dance;

A time to cast away stones, and a time to gather stones together;

A time to embrace, and a time to refrain from embracing;

A time to get, and a time to lose;

A time to keep, and a time to cast away;

A time to rend, and a time to sew;

A time to keep silence, and a time to speak;

A time to love, and a time to hate;

A time of war, and a time of peace."

Ecclesiastes 3:2-8

I would add but one thing to the list: "A time to parent, and a time to grandparent." And if you have children—or grandchildren—the time is now.

Someone once asked a mother of 11 children, "How do you find time to take care of all your children?"

"Well," she replied, "when I had my first baby, I realized one child took all my time. So I figured a few more children couldn't take that much more time!"

Let's face it—it takes time to parent. Just the hours a mother has to spend in child-generated housework can boggle the mind. Someone calculated that a mother with three children has spent on the average more than 18,000 hours in child-generated housework by the time her children are 18 years of age—that is, housework she would not have had without the children.

New parents often are overwhelmed by how much time a baby takes. First, there is the time for his physical care—his diapering, feeding, bathing, dressing; time putting him to sleep, comforting his crying; and time spent waiting in a pediatrician's office. But a growing child also demands more of their time in other respects. He needs time to be played with, time for talking, time to be cuddled and to be rocked.

Time and attention spell love to the baby. There is no substitute. How can a parent find the time necessary to give the child what he needs to grow up to be healthy, happy, and satisfied? Here are some suggestions:

Take advantage of the time you must spend with the child and make it meaningful, loving time. For example, after a month or so you become so adept at changing diapers that probably you could do this chore blindfolded. But instead of putting your mind in neutral or planning next week's menus, think about how you could make this time more meaningful to your baby. Talk to her. Nibble on her toes. Tickle her tummy. Explain what you are doing. Touch and name different body parts. If you change a dozen diapers a day, that is 12 extra times a day you can have a special playtime together.

Include the child in your activities. When you are reading, rock the baby and read aloud. When cooking dinner, carry the baby on your back. When sewing, put the playpen next to you so you can interact between stitches. If you like to jog, jog behind the stroller.

Do not spend much money on mechanical toys, automatic swings, fancy infant seats, and educational cribs. If you do, you will want the baby to use them as much as possible, thus robbing the child of your time together. Leaving a baby alone for hours in a fancy crib does not build IQ or character. It is the interaction with people that really counts. Why substitute second best when your baby can have you—the best?

Fathers, if your work schedule does not allow time at home when your preschooler is awake, try rearranging the child's sleeping schedule. When my brother was on the police force, he worked afternoons and evenings, arriving home about 10:00 p.m.—past the regular bedtime for most children. But his wife and child adjusted their schedules so they would not be deprived of their special time with daddy. Supper was served at 10:00 p.m., next came the routine playtime with daddy, and then the whole family slept until ten or so the next morning.

And what if your child does not want to spend time with you? It may happen, especially if you are home so seldom you seem like a stranger. This occurred to my busy physician friend, who often was unable to be home at his son's bedtime. When he tried to give Chad a goodnight hug or kiss, Chad resisted. Only mother was allowed to tuck him into bed.

So one night as she was tucking Chad into bed, father secretly crept into the room and tossed a rubber ball into his son's bed. Surprised, his son laughed and tossed it back. Over came the ball again. And thus evolved a nightly ritual, with the projectiles ranging from slippers and socks one night to soft toys and animals the next. A friend once asked Chad, "Does your daddy read stories to you at bedtime?"

"No," he replied with a gleam in his eye, "he just throws things at me!"

You too can find creative ways to spend fun time together. And before you know it your child will be begging for more.

Children of all ages need special attention. One evening my friend Marilyn was in the midst of preparing gravy for dinner when her teenage son rushed into the kitchen, shouting, "Mom, come outside quickly! I've got something to show you."

The preparation of gravy has a critical point when the gravy must be stirred in order to have a smooth consistency. Marilyn, who is a gourmet cook and relishes the thought of a perfect dinner, was at that critical preparation point and almost said, "Can't you wait a minute? I've got to finish stirring the gravy." But an inner sense said, "Go!" After all, it had been weeks since her son had asked her anything—or even wanted to be with the family.

So she turned off the stove, removed the gravy, and went outside. Her son pointed to the western horizon and exclaimed, "Mom, look at that sunset! Isn't that the most beautiful thing you've ever seen?" They both watched until the last rays disappeared.

A wasted moment? It may have seemed so, if smooth gravy is the thing you value most in life. But as this mother said, "I'd eat lumpy gravy every night of the week to have that kind of daily experience with my teenager. After all, gravy soon disappears, but the relationship I establish with my son can last a lifetime.'' Remember, pleasant time spent with the child is never wasted.

James Boswell, the biographer of Samuel Johnson, often talked about the day his father took him fishing and how important it had been to him as a young lad. A curious researcher decided to check the father's diary to see whether Boswell's father had recorded a similar reaction to that particular event. And there opposite the date, these words were penned, ''Gone fishing today with my son; a day wasted.''

It is the time we ''waste'' with (and for) our children that will assure a good relationship with them and convince them of our love. This time has to be given joyfully, with our wholehearted interest in their affairs. Never let your child think that you would *rather* be doing something else (although you may *need* to do something else) or that you feel you are wasting your time when you are with him.

Your time given willingly and lovingly is the best gift you can give to your child. It's a gift no money can buy. Give it today—and give it generously. You can find the time, if you really want to.

Teaching Your Own Preschool Children

A father once complained, "Why do I always end up having to help Billy with his homework?"

"Be thankful you can help," his wife replied, "next year you may not know the answers!"

Children grow up so quickly. And it's true, they soon outgrow our limited skills and abilities, moving on to others for special instruction.

Yet, there is a special joy that comes when working side by side with your children as Joseph worked with Jesus in the carpenter's shop. And what better method of "training up a child in the way he should go" (Proverbs 22:6) then by dedicating those first few years to teaching your own preschool children?

"Mommy, mommy, come outside quickly! You won't believe the surprise I have for you." It was my 5-year-old daughter, Kim, who was calling, followed by 4-year-old Kari saying, "Yeah, Mommy, it's real neat."

Well, at least my curiosity was aroused enough to leave my letter half typed and follow the girls. Outside Kim raced to her bicycle, from which I had just recently removed the training wheels. I must have run behind her for miles, holding on to the seat, trying to teach her how to balance it. Just this morning Kim had almost started crying over the frustrating experience, and I was beginning to doubt she would ever master it! I watched in disbelief as she got the pedals in just the proper place, put one foot on, and gave a little push with the other, wobbled unsteadily for a second, and then rode her bike the whole length of the driveway, even maneuvering the ninety-degree turn.

I changed my mind right then. The joy of seeing Kim's exhilarating excitement of achieving the almost impossible was worth every minute and more that I had spent helping her. Yes, I had to admit—being my child's preschool teacher was a satisfying job.

It all began the summer before as I was planning my fall schedule. Naturally, the girls would go to nursery school three mornings a week while I taught my classes. But what about 2-year-old Kevin? One of the requirements for nursery school entrance was being potty trained—and he didn't qualify. My first choice was to keep the children together, and so on the spur of the moment I asked the girls what they would prefer: go to nursery school or have Mommy stay home and be their teacher. With screams of delight, hugging, kissing, and jumping up and down they said, "Mommy!" After that kind of reaction, I couldn't disappoint them.

I rearranged my schedule so that I would be away only two afternoons a week, saving mornings for the children. Long-time experience had taught me that mornings were when young children were most receptive.

We decided to start preschool the day after Labor Day. When the day arrived, I had so many other things to do, such as canning four boxes of peaches, that I almost didn't start. It would be so easy to wait until I was not so busy.

Where was my will power? I decided then and there, no matter what I had to do, that my children came first and I would act like a teacher. When the first day of school comes, the teacher is there. I would be too.

I didn't realize how important it was for me to make this commitment, until a number of weeks later. Kim had some six-inch squares of material that had been given to her by a friend, and she announced one morning, "I want to make a hat for Kari." She had no idea how to sew, so I thought it was a passing fancy until she got a needle and thread and asked me to thread it for her. If I had not made the commitment of being her teacher, I'm sure I would have left her alone to struggle or said, "It's too hard; don't even try," or I would have done it myself. Instead I realized we both were heading for a frustrating experience if we tried to do it by hand, so I took her on my lap and taught her how to use my sewing machine.

It was amazing how quickly she learned to backstitch to lock the threads, how to guide the material through, keeping fingers well out of the way of the needle, how to lift the sewing foot and cut the threads on the back of the machine. In no time the hat was finished and even Kevin wanted to wear it. It was only that commitment I had made earlier that made me spend all the extra time teaching.

Every parent is his child's teacher whether or not he wants the job. I had always taught my children as I worked around the house; I had always read and sung to them. But making a commitment that I was their sole preschool teacher and would not rely on anyone else, led me to spend the extra time with my children—time I was sure I didn't have.

I believe young children learn primarily through their play and should be allowed the freedom to play out-of-doors and to choose the activities they enjoy most.

And yet children can be guided and given activities that will help them in their development, for example, practical duties, lessons from nature, and Bible stories. I wrote down the things I wanted my children to learn during the year. Then I printed on a 3 by 5 card each activity that would help teach these things. I thought up about ten activities the first day, and each day I thought of a couple more to add to the list. For example:

Go to the library and get twenty-five books.
Clean room.
Learn telephone number: 792-2412.
Make bird feeder.
Fold clothes.
Make a picture book; tell stories about each picture.
Learn A, B, and C on the piano.
Listen to story about honesty.
Make granola.
Practice roller-skating.

The children loved it. Each day they eagerly waited for preschool time so they could sort through the cards and select the ones they would like to do. The cards that were perpetual duties, such as "cleaning room," we left in the pile. Other cards that were a one-time experience, the children signed their names on when they were completed and we put them in a special box.

I got most of my ideas for activities by listening to the children express what they wanted to do or what they wanted to learn about. On my shelves I had a number of activity books for children. It's good to glance through them for new ideas.

Don't limit your teaching to the cards. Use your common sense and take advantage of every opportunity during the day to teach, whether or not the activity is on a card.

The children usually did three or four cards a day. If they were not interested in anything I'd written down, I asked them, "What would you like to do?" I would then write it down and we were on our way.

Sometimes when I share with other parents what I did with my own children, they say, "Well, you used to be a teacher, so you know what and how to teach, but I've no idea what to do." I encourage them just to try, and then to give them a guide, I recorded my experiences in the book, *Teaching Your Own Preschool Children.* (Doubleday, 1980.)

I have never enjoyed my children so much as I did during that preschool year when I was their teacher. Child rearing has many satisfactions, but when you really sign up for the job and become your child's teacher, no salary can bring the satisfaction that comes to you from watching your child finally accomplish something you helped him with. Every mother can enroll her children in the home school with no tuition—all you need is a willing teacher.

If I can do it, you can!

Prime-time Parenting

When parents work outside the home, or find themselves extra busy, they must learn to take advantage of what I call "prime-time hours" with their children. The admonition to remember is, "Withhold not good from them to whom it is due, when it is in the power of thine hand to do it." (Proverbs 3:27.)

Here is a busy parent's guide to spending quality time together with God's kids.

I've always been a working mother. My husband, Jan, is a working father. But we are both striving to be more than working parents. Our goal is to become "prime-time parents," parents who are vitally interested in maintaining positive relationships with our children—Kim, Kari, and Kevin—even though our schedules permit less than a 24-hour-a-day vigil.

We've found that it is possible to combine a paying job—even a demanding career—with the job of parenting, and raise healthy, happy, competent children. There are no magic formulas, but as prime-time parents we now consider every minute with our children prime time to communicate love, interest, and care.

One winter day I put on an old coat and shoved my hands into the pockets. What was that I felt? I pulled out a crumpled piece of paper, unfolded it and discovered this note. "Dear Mommy, How are you? I am fine. I love you. Love, Kim (you know who)."

Pockets are marvelous inventions. Pockets are meant to put things into; they are meant to be filled. Pockets are for surprises. Time has pockets too, minutes or hours here and there that can be used creatively. Prime-time parents cultivate the habit of filling every empty pocket of time with love.

Most parents work hard to provide their children with the necessities, as well as a few luxuries, of life. But possessions are only of secondary importance, while parental love is primary.

Jim Andrews, a successful businessman, loved his wife and two children deeply. He believed in giving them the very best: summer camps, private boarding schools, trips abroad. In order to afford these luxuries he worked long hours.

When his daughter, Marie, showed an interest in playing a harp, he purchased the best instrument available. But when she played at a recital, Andrews was unable to attend because of business commitments. Larry, his son, made the Little League team and Andrews purchased new uniforms for the entire squad. But he couldn't justify time off to watch Larry play.

When Marie and Larry finished high school, Andrews' dream for his children began to fall apart. During her first semester of college, Marie announced that she wanted to get married. Larry refused to go to college, so Andrews purchased a new Jaguar for him and extracted the promise that he would complete at least one year—but Larry passed only two courses.

When Andrews confronted both children with his anger and disappointment, they replied, "Why should you care what we do? You don't love us." "What do you mean, I don't love you? I've given you everything you have," was the father's anguished reply.

What went wrong? Andrews worked hard to show his family just how much he loved them. But his message wasn't heard because you can't say "I love you" with things. It is your "presence," not your "presents," that expresses your love. This does not mean that you must spend every spare minute with your child. However, when you are not there, you must continue to communicate love and to convince your children that your absence does not mean other people are more important to you than they are.

From experience and observation, we've learned several ways you can fill your children's pockets with love:

Play games with your children. Get involved at their level. Starting at birth, play the "I'll touch your nose, tickle your tummy and pedal your feet" games that mirror growing skills. Toddlers love the "chase me but don't catch me," "peek-a-boo" and "make funny faces" games. Preschoolers enjoy pretend games like "let's play house" or "fireman," or "going to the restaurant." School-age children enjoy organized games like basketball, baseball and table tennis, and some teenagers favor high-powered games like "sit down Mom and Dad and help me build this computer." The key to success is to be responsive to your child's abilities and creative enough to make a game out of whatever you are doing together.

Involve them in your activities. A colleague who often goes to Washington, D. C., on business takes each of his teenagers once a year. While Dad attends meetings, the teenager visits the Smithsonian or sees other interesting sights.

Each evening they do something special together. This prime time with Dad has been a memorable experience for each.

Do you go birding? Why not take your child along and teach him how to spot certain species? If photography is your thing, introduce your child to the darkroom. But remember his level of capabilities. He may not be able to sit through a long meeting, hike ten miles a day, or fish on a quiet lake without rocking the boat, but with a little modification you should be able to make memorable occasions for both of you.

Enjoy each child individually. A teacher once asked her class what happiness was. One child replied, "Happiness is when I go walk on the dunes with Dad. Nobody else, just him and me."

Finding time to spend alone with a child is difficult when families are large or when children are born close together. One busy minister, father of six, solved this problem by scheduling bedtimes at half-hour intervals, then using the time to talk over the day's events, to read aloud and to listen to each child's prayers.

Do the unexpected. How often we miss the beauty and richness of life because we are locked into routines. I once read about a father who bundled up his sleeping seven-year-old son and carried him out into the darkness. As the boy's sleep-filled eyes began to focus on his surroundings, the father shouted, "Look!" There in the sky the little boy saw a star leap from its place and fall toward the ground. Then another star fell, and another and another. The boy never forgot that night—and he determined that he would do the same some August evening when his son was seven.

Keep a "why-not" list of interesting, crazy things to do with or for your children. Why not milk a cow? Go up in a balloon, or take a helicopter ride? Visit the local radio station? Sit on the roof and watch the moon come up? Camp out in your back yard with sleeping bags and a campfire?

When your children make simple requests like "Can we stop by to see the Cassidys?" or "Daddy, may we feed the ducks at the park?" do the unexpected. Say, "Why not?"

Open doors for your child. After winning a tournament, a teenager was asked when she became interested in tennis. She thought for a moment and replied, "It was the day my father gave it to me." A reporter asked, "You mean, when your father bought you a racket?" "No," she replied, "It was the day Dad took off from work and played with me. That was the day he gave me tennis."

Opening doors for your children means giving them more options in life, and increasing their understanding and appreciation of events and people. Share a good book and open the door of quality writing to your children. Open the door to the artistic world by visiting art museums and galleries. Your children may not want to walk through every door. That's fine. Just keep opening, and allow them to enter those they choose.

Communicate. Studies on runaways suggest the most important way a parent can help a troubled adolescent is to listen. Running away is a desperate attempt to communicate. Here are some guidelines:

1. Stop what you are doing and show an interest in your child's conversation.

2. Don't correct her speech when she is talking to you or cut her off prematurely by arguing with her point of view.

3. Listen with a soft touch. Don't laugh, belittle, tear down or make it more difficult for a child to open up his heart and ideas to you.

4. Encourage your child to share his world with you. One

way is to have a talk-about-it bowl in the kitchen, where children can put objects, clippings or articles that they would like to talk about at dinner time. Even the most reluctant child is likely to speak up at a show-and-tell meal.

5. Have a weekly family council. Ask each member to bring up problems and discuss changes that might be made.

6. Allow expression of negative feelings. When children say, "I hate you," acknowledge their feelings by saying something like, "You *are* angry," rather than punishing them.

A mother I know had returned to college to finish a degree. One morning she got up early, folded the wash and put it in a basket. When next she looked, the clothes were a jumble. Her 17-year-old had been looking for his blue shirt. She was angry that her son would act so irresponsibly when she was so busy and she realized that if she didn't do something, she would be angry all day. "Bill," she said, "I'm angry at the way you left the ironing basket."

"Oh, sorry Mom," he replied. He refolded the garments, then gave her a kiss and said, "Don't study too hard . . . and by the way, thanks for washing my shirt." Now she could enjoy her day because she had communicated her feelings and had allowed her son to tuck a little love into *her* day.

Prepare for the times you're away. Young children often think that Mom and Dad don't love them when they go away, so take the time to prepare your children for your absence: make sure they understand the reasons for the separation; arrange for quality care from someone they enjoy; and plan ways to fill your children's pockets of time with love while you're away.

The most difficult part of the day can be bedtime. One mother solved this problem by reading stories to her child via a tape recorder. Her daughter was reminded of Mom's love at the end of every day when she heard her voice saying, "I love you and miss you. So snuggle up in your warm, cozy bed. I'm going to blow you a kiss. Did you catch it?"

Take advantage of prime prime-times. There are certain times when your presence or absence will have a greater-than-usual impact. If it is impossible for you to be home when your child arrives from school, you can still make homecoming special. A warm note is a good welcome. One mother takes a few minutes one morning a week to lay out a treasure hunt with a treat hidden at the end. The child never knows which day to expect this surprise, which adds to the effectiveness.

Any time a child is performing in public is a prime time to show love and support. Applause from strangers is not nearly as meaningful as the approval of Mom and Dad. No matter how small your child's role, your presence is important.

If I could choose only 15 minutes a day to spend with my children, it would be bedtime. This is when I listen to my children's prayers, tuck them in with a hug and a kiss, then linger after lights are off to chat, rub backs and snuggle—if they feel like it.

Remember, love does not spoil a child; too little discipline spoils a child. Love does not mean allowing wrong-doing, fostering dependence, or showering a child with gifts, bribes and rewards. It means building a child's feelings of self-worth. So start today. Fill every pocket of your child's time with a heaping amount of love.

Make Your Homecoming Count

I love this passage, "Let not your heart be troubled: ye believe in God, believe also in me. In my Father's house are many mansions: if it were not so, I would have told you. I go to prepare a place for you. And if I go and prepare a place for you, I will come again, and receive you unto myself; that where I am, there ye may be also." (John 14:1-3.)

What joy and anticipation I feel to know that God is preparing for my homecoming to heaven! Why, right now He may be putting the finishing touches on my water-front home while Gabriel's polishing up his trumpet to announce the arrival! It makes me feel wanted and welcome and very, very special. I can hardly wait until the Lord comes in all His glory to take us home with Him.

If arrival time in heaven is so wonderful that every stop will be pulled, why shouldn't arrival times into our homes (which should be little heavens on earth) be something special?

With thought, planning and creativity you can make each homecoming an unforgettable event.

Down with the briefcase. Off with the shoes. Flop on the couch. Exhausted. Kids yell, "Hi." The electric train drowns your feeble reply. Wife—she's around. The whine of the vacuum confirms that. Why bother competing? Why bother? Here's why . . . Unless *you* initiate a meaningful relationship with your family in the next minute or two you have just scored the lowest possible homecoming score—a two-pointer. With the investment of only a little more time and thought it could have been a 15-pointer and you could have been well on your way to making your evening at home a gold-medal experience.

Do you want to be a winner? Here is how you can transform low quality time into meaningful, loving relationships. Love is best communicated at close range when you are together. But that's not always possible. The next best thing is to let your loved ones know you are thinking about them even while you are away. Pick up the laundry on the way home, surprise her with a fresh strawberry pie, call him mid-morning and say, "I can't keep my mind off you —just had to say Hello." Communicating love "long distance" is worth one point. It's what I call mental proximity.

Physical proximity is worth two points. Just being home is important. It suggests that you care for your family enough at least to come home to them. But it is what you do after you walk through the door that really determines the meaningfulness of your homecoming.

Here is how you can make your homecoming a 15-pointer. Give yourself three points for talking with your family. Be willing to listen as well as express. Don't just spout cliches (Hi, I'm home. How are you? What's for dinner?) but thoughtfully communicate. (I love coming home to you. You're so bright and cheerful. This is the best part of my day. You really know how to make me feel ten feet tall.)

You get four points for eye contact—actually focusing

on the other person—and five points for physical contact. Don't forget the hug and kiss, or the rub of the back. Touch is essential for top-quality relationships. Now put it all together and you can have a 15-point homecoming.

"Hi, honey, I'm home" (2 points for physical proximity), "Hey, you look terrific. I'm the luckiest person in the world" (3 points for talking). "Mmmm, you feel good, too" (5 points for touching—as you give your spouse a squeeze and a nibble on the ear). Then as you focus on each other (4 points for looking) you say, "Called you about three—(1 point for thinking about a person while you were away)—but didn't get an answer. Thought you'd like to hear that the contract from Ross and Company came through. . . ."

But don't stop here. If you have children waiting in the next room, give them a 15-pointer, too. Tell them you thought about them during the day. Then focus on them and listen to their needs. Top the occasion with a physical expression of affection—a hug, pat on the back, or a ruffle of the hair.

And there you have it. Just a little thoughtfulness, a little touch, and a little extra focused attention is what makes the difference between an average, nonmeaningful homecoming and a memorable one.

Jan specializes in 15-point homecomings. One night he called, "Children, come quickly. I'm going to give your mother an Italian kiss." (Guess who came quickly!) I wondered what my husband was going to do. Jan took me in his arms, swept me off my feet and gave me a memorable kiss. "Wow," said Kim, "I want one, too!" "Me, too," Kari and Kevin chorused. So Jan went down the line giving them each their Italian kiss.

Another time Jan put a ladder to the roof and asked the children to climb up. After we were all standing on the roof, he pointed to the horizon. "Look, the moon is just coming up!" We had never stood on the roof and watched the moon come up. Neither had the neighbors watched the Kuzmas stand on the roof and watch the moon come up. But it was an experience we will never forget.

Time is precious. Tomorrow when you come home to your family don't waste a minute. Plan ahead so that you and your family can experience a 15-point homecoming. You'll find it worth the extra effort.

The Working Mother's Challenge

Loving, nurturing and teaching God's kids is more than a full-time responsibility.

Realizing the time-consuming nature of parenting, is it possible to be a good parent and also work outside the home? The virtuous woman in Proverbs 31 did. She bought real estate, planted vineyards and carried on a garment business, **without neglecting her home responsibilities.**

Working away from home may never be ideal, but for many women it's necessary—and it's a real challenge.

Parenting is the most important career you will ever be called upon to perform. It takes time, creativity and lots of energy. So not every woman will choose to become a working mother. Other mothers will feel called to perform a special work outside the home and enjoy the fulfillment it brings. And being realistic—many will need to work just to make ends meet. Obviously, a dedicated mother will make her family her top priority whether or not she works.

If you choose to be a working mother you will have accepted an extraordinary challenge. But you can have a career and be a good parent, too. It isn't easy. Nothing really worthwhile is easy! Having a formula for success, however, will help. Here is my recommendation: You must make sure your family, and your employer, knows that your family comes first, and then work to become indispensable to your job and dispensable to your family.

It sounds complicated doesn't it? But it's really not. Let's take a step at a time.

Make sure your family comes first. When children feel that something else holds first place in your life they will constantly strive for that valued position. They will test your love, argue, fight, complain, and resent whatever fills that number-one place. Even husbands can grow jealous if they feel you're neglecting them for the job!

To alleviate these feelings, you must convince your family of their prime importance. One way is to be with them when it really counts. Every family has special times when togetherness is particularly important—mealtime, worship, after-school hours, bedtime, birthdays, holidays, special school activities, performance times, and so on. Select the priority times for your family and be there!

When family members feel excluded from a major and important part of your life, they tend to resent it. So whenever possible, include your family in your job. Let them visit your place of work—see you in action. If possible, let your children help with small projects. When I'm facing a deadline on the preparation of a manuscript, my children enjoy pushing the button on the copy machine and collating the pages. At other times they can help by being good—and quiet—so I can concentrate.

Your employer should also understand the high value you place on your family. This doesn't mean you will neglect the job. In fact, because you value your family you will actually work to become indispensable to your job. (But that's step two!) Employers know that employees with satisfying home relationships can be more efficient and creative than those who are bogged down with family bickering, misunderstandings and resentment. Family problems zap the emotional energy needed to be an indispensable employee.

Become indispensable to the job. After things are going well with the family, it's time to begin on step two: Making sure you become indispensable to the job.

Crystal was a skilled secretary—no doubt about that, as she typed letter-perfect memos at 140 words per minute. But she worked mechanically. It was her job—nothing more. She did only what was necessary. When work was slow she pulled out her needlepoint. When work piled up and a crisis demanded overtime, she politely excused herself. "My job description says my hours are from eight to five," she told her boss. She was frequently late because of babysitting problems. When her child became ill, pediatrician appointments interfered with office hours. Crystal made no attempt to make up this time. When a mother-daughter day was planned at her daughter's school, Crystal asked her boss for time off. Her boss, a kind, understanding person, was clearly not happy about the request. He suggested that she look for another job that would allow her a more flexible work schedule.

Lenore was not as good a typist, but from her first hour on the job her boss was aware of her enthusiasm for her work and her dedication. Lenore was a working mother with preschool and school-age children. Her family/job conflicts exceeded Crystal's. But when it came to the job, she was one hundred percent there, ready and willing to go the extra mile. When the volume of work piled up, she came in early and worked late. And her dedication paid off. She was liked, she was needed, and she was considered an indispensable employee. Once her track record was established—and it didn't take long—Lenore did not hesitate to ask for small benefits. "I'd like to take the afternoon off. My son's class has a field trip and he wants me to go along. The statements have been mailed and your latest tape has been transcribed. I'll be happy to come in early tomorrow morning if anything comes up that needs immediate attention."

"Sure, take the afternoon off," her boss replied. "And don't worry about coming in early. You deserve a break."

Why did Crystal's boss and Lenore's boss respond as they did? What made the difference? It was indispensability. Lenore had become indispensable to the job. Her boss viewed her as a valuable asset to the business, one he did not want to lose. It was to his advantage to make the job as attractive as possible in order to keep employees like Lenore.

College is the prime time to begin working on becoming indispensable to your future job. Get all the training possible before you start your family. Take that advanced degree. Put in the long hours of study and the extra lab time while you're single and don't have the added responsibilities of a home and family. Highly skilled and educated workers are valuable, indispensable employees.

Before the family comes along, you should try to reach a satisfying career level. Small children demand and need your time. You may find it impossible to climb the career ladder and be a super parent, too. If you need to pace your career—and most conscientious parents do—then you won't feel that your family is depriving you of career opportunities.

Become dispensable to your family. And now the final step: You must become dispensable to your family. This doesn't mean that you are no longer important to them. It simply means that your family can survive without disruption and pain when your job becomes particularly demanding. Dispensability is only possible if you are willing to share your child-care and other home responsibilities. Contrary to a widely held notion, the best mothers aren't necessarily those who handle all the child-care and home responsibilities alone. Quality and diversity can be compatible. This is certainly true when a father is encouraged to share these tasks. Relatives and friends can also make an important contribution. Even your children can benefit from interactions with others.

In addition, teach your children self-sufficiency. If they can learn to handle various chores on their own, you'll be able to spend your free time with your children in enjoyable ways, rather than tying up that time in a constant round of necessary and routine activities. If your children can prepare simple meals, you won't feel guilty if the boss occasionally asks you to come in early or work overtime. You can feel confident that the children can pack their own lunches or prepare supper for the family.

Don't kill your family's willingness to help by expecting perfection. Appreciate whatever help you receive. Encourage them to learn from their mistakes. It's the effort and the motives that count. With practice, their products and skills will improve and you'll find their help a valuable asset when juggling two careers.

Yes, it is possible to have a career and be a good parent, too. Put your family first, become indispensable to your job and dispensable to your family. Accept the challenge and design your life so you can experience the satisfying, fulfilling life God intended for you to find within your family.

The Problem of Guilt

Guilt is the emotion we experience when we dislike our behavior; when we know we have done something wrong. Every parent at times feels pangs of guilt for not being the kind of parent God's kids deserve.

Guilt can be healthy—if we recognize the emotion immediately and make the changes necessary so we don't have to continue feeling guilty. But if we continue to do nothing, guilt grows and weighs us down with negative thoughts which affects our behavior. "Cast thy burden (your guilt) upon the Lord, and he shall sustain thee," is good advice for the guilt-ridden parent. (Psalm 55:22.)

The problem is when guilt is irrational. For example, we continue to feel guilty over past wrongs even after we have made changes and asked for forgiveness. Sometimes parents blame themselves for the bad choices their children make, not realizing that God holds everyone (even children and teenagers) responsible for their own behavior. All parents make mistakes, but children can choose whether or not they will allow those mistakes to affect their behavior. Remember, God always forgives. "Come now, and let us reason together, saith the Lord: though your sins be as scarlet, they shall be as white as snow; though they be red like crimson, they shall be as wool." (Isaiah 1:18.) If God forgives us, why shouldn't we forgive ourselves?

Guilt is a major problem of parents, especially working mothers. They feel guilty about working while their children are small; guilty about leaving them with baby sitters and in day-care centers; guilty about their absence when baby says his first word or takes her first step; guilty about their older children coming home to an empty house; guilty about being unable to participate in the children's daytime school activities; guilty about feeling too tired to enjoy the children in the evening; guilty about becoming angry and yelling and spending precious time together in conflict; guilty about not having time to make fancy birthday cakes and party costumes; guilty that the house never seems spic-and-span. The list is endless.

Guilt is debilitating, discouraging, and defeating if no effort is made to eradicate the feelings. Yet the advice "Don't feel guilty" is difficult to accept. However unrealistic these feelings may be in a broader context, if you share them they are both genuine and painful for you. The only solution is to recognize guilt and reduce it by taking positive action.

If you repress too many negative feelings, you won't be able to experience fully the more positive emotions of happiness and joy. But if you recognize your negative feelings, you can work with those feelings rather than letting them mount until the frustration level becomes unbearable.

What happens when you bottle up negative guilt feelings? Let's consider a typical, imaginary situation. You have had a particularly hard week. The boss demanded that you work overtime, and you didn't get home until after the children's bedtime. You feel guilty that you haven't spent more time with the children. On Monday you realize you're beginning to feel depressed. You can hardly get up in the morning and get the children off to school. You arrive at work full of resentment toward the job and toward your boss, who makes so many demands. Because you feel guilty, depressed, and resentful, you can't seem to get organized, and your efficiency is significantly reduced. By 5:00 p.m. you still have a stack of work on your desk and you're feeling guilty about your workload. You come home frustrated and yell at the children for innocently giggling and goofing around. They stop immediately and put their arms around you, saying, "We're sorry, Mom." You push them away. "I just need to be alone," you tell them. Later, when the house is quiet, you begin to feel guilty about screaming at the children. Is there no way out of this endless cycle of guilt?

Now, replay the scene with a few modifications. When you wake up on Monday face those feelings of depression and guilt. After thinking about some possible solutions you make up your mind: *no more overtime.* It just cuts too deeply into your time with the family. Making that decision is a relief, although you're somewhat scared to tell the boss. You kiss the kids goodbye with a cheery "See you at five." When you get to work you confront your boss immediately. "I felt guilty all last week because I couldn't spend more time with my children, so I can't work overtime anymore. I'm willing to work lunch hours, but my children need me after school. They are disappointed when I'm late. I hope you can understand my decision."

What was the difference between the two scenarios? In the first you felt guilty, but you didn't do anything about the feelings, and they continued to build up. In the second you recognized the feelings and took constructive action. As a result, the feelings disappeared.

Often parents with the most training in developmental

psychology and human behavior feel the most guilty. They know what effective parenting entails, and can easily see the disparity between their behavior and that elusive goal. Research findings or information from a best-selling book can generate guilt about past behavior toward the children—which at this point cannot be changed. For example, one book may advise you to forget about toilet training, because the child will train himself when he is really ready. A second book notes that 2-year-olds can and should be toilet trained. The third book says you can toilet train your child (when he's ready) in twenty-four hours. The first book may generate guilt about being too hard on your child. The second book makes you feel guilty if you were too soft. The third book encourages guilt if you weren't able to do it in twenty-four hours.

The only possible benefit of considering your past mistakes is to help you make better decisions in the future. Parents need to realize that they are going to make mistakes in their job of child rearing. They may become angry and impatient; they may demand too much of their children; they may not always be there when their children need them. Learn to say "I'm sorry," and sincerely try to do better the next time. It is not the occasional mistake that shapes children's lives. It is the prevailing attitude of the parents and the atmosphere of the home.

Working mothers often blame themselves (or the fact that they are working) for their children's problems. Friends, neighbors, and relatives can increase such guilt feelings by wagging their tongues and fingers disapprovingly: "If only she'd stay home and be a mother she wouldn't have problems with her children." Research does not support this idea. Nonworking mothers have as many problems with their children as working mothers. If a mother is happy, whether or not she is working, her children tend to be fairly well adjusted.

An outside job may actually be a necessary escape for a mother who can't cope with her child's problem behavior. Work may be an oasis for you if you have an extremely difficult child, such as a handicapped child. You can return to your child with renewed enthusiasm and energy. The responsibility of child rearing is sometimes overwhelming. You should not feel guilty when you must ask others to help.

If you continue to feel guilty about working, carefully consider the reasons. Does it contradict your childhood values? Values *can* change. If work is not an economic necessity, consider part-time employment or a less demanding job when the children are young and need you most. If you have to work, then dwell on the positive aspects of the job rather than the negative.

Does your spouse disapprove of the fact that you're working when the children are small? If he does, and you still choose to work, make a pact to be honest, open-minded, and respectful of each other. Then try this exercise. Make a list of the negative and positive aspects of your job. Be specific. Ask your spouse to do the same, then compare the two lists. Look at the positive side first, and try to agree on as many positive points as possible. Then compare the negative side of the list. Brainstorm possible solutions for each negative point. Quitting would be one answer. Continuing to work without any changes would be the opposite extreme. Be willing to compromise. Consider some of these ideas: part-time work; hiring a housekeeper; fixing meals ahead of time; arranging a more flexible work schedule; taking a less demanding job; working closer to home or moving closer to work; hiring a live-in baby sitter; coming home promptly after work.

Do your relatives, friends, or fellow church members

disapprove of working mothers? If so, then you must evaluate the importance you place on their opinion and decide to what degree their beliefs should influence your life. At times you must learn to say, "I am unique. My situation is unique. I will do the best I can for my immediate family." The opinions of the church, neighbors, and relatives are *less* important than your own feelings about what is best for your family's happiness and well-being.

Do you feel guilty because you don't like your job and would prefer to stay home? If you are unhappy and have a choice, *quit*—if you are sure that nonworking status will bring happiness. In many cases, however, a new job will alleviate such feelings.

Is your guilt caused by exhaustion or your inability to find the time to meet all your household obligations? You may be trying to do too much. Hire help or ask your family to provide more help. Be specific in explaining your needs. Get to bed an hour earlier—whether or not your "homework" is done. Make sure that you are physically fit. Begin a regular program to improve your health habits.

Do you feel guilty because you sense that your children are receiving inadequate child care? If so, thoughtfully write down the specific incidents that justify your feeling. You may want to counsel with others to check whether your perception is realistic. Then if the situation cannot be remedied, your only option may be to quit work until good care is found. If you continue to work when you feel your child is definitely receiving substandard care, it will be almost impossible to relieve your guilt feelings. You cannot continue to live happily with this conflict brewing inside you.

However you choose to deal with guilt, do *not* allow occasional guilt feelings to affect your parenting. The following list includes the most common child-rearing mistakes made by guilty parents.

1. *Overprotecting the child.* "I'm not home very often, so I want to compensate by being with my child whenever I'm home and carefully monitoring her time when I'm not home." Children thrive on age-related independence—not smothering.

2. *Giving unnecessary gifts.* Some parents believe that they can make up for their absence by giving gifts. Presents never take the place of parental presence.

3. *Giving in to demands.* Children often play on a parent's guilt feelings to get what they want. Parents fall into this trap by trying to meet every desire and whim of their child. In such situations the child runs the home—and it's not a happy place for either parent or child.

4. *Feeling sorry for the child.* "Oh, you poor dear. I feel so sorry for you when I have to work. You don't have a mommy here when you get home from school." This attitude only encourages the child to feel sorry for himself. Instead, help your child see the benefits that can be derived from your work.

5. *Allowing the child to escape home responsibilities.* "After all, this poor child has a mommy who works, so the least I can do is to make it up to him by doing his chores and picking up after him." Balderdash!

6. *Ignoring misbehavior.* "I don't want to cross my child, since I'm home so little. I'll leave that to the babysitter. I want my child to like me, so I'll just ignore the bad things he does." This attitude is particularly dangerous because you are encouraging your child to exhibit more of this antisocial behavior.

Children need parents who are willing to parent—and that includes healthy doses of both love and discipline. Don't deny your child his valuable training because you feel guilty about working. Instead, do your best, keep happy, apologize when you fail, and plan ways to avoid repeating the mistake. Follow these four steps:

1. *Count your blessings.* Each day try to learn new ways to fill your life with enjoyment, fun, and contentment. Don't focus on the negative aspects of life, focus on the positive. Count the blessings that work brings into your life and the lives of your chidren; new contacts and friends, new challenges; a focus for your creativity; new ideas to share with your children; colleagues whom your children enjoy; a whole new set of "uncles" and "aunts"; a broadening of interests; and extra income. Children benefit by seeing their parents take on different roles willingly—Dad doing the cooking and Mom attending a convention. As children become older they benefit by feeling needed. They can be important contributing members to their family by carrying more and more of the home responsibilities.

2. *Realize you can't be perfect.* No parent is perfect—at least not for long. Work toward this goal, as expressed in a jingle adapted from the Danish poet Piet Heim.

> The principle of perfect parenting is simple to express.
> Err, and err, and err again, but less, and less, and less.

3. *Stay on the cutting edge.* Try to minimize pain, conflict, jealousy, and boredom by solving problems as soon as they develop. Look for the first signs of dissatisfaction. Talk to the person involved immediately. "You look as if what I did made you jealous (or whatever). What can I do to avoid such misunderstanding in the future?" Be willing to apologize first. The words "Forgive me" are often met by a response like "It really wasn't all your fault." Then you are in a good position to solve the problem at an early stage. If you are busy solving problems as they arise, there is little time left for guilt. When you allow problems to build, they seem insurmountable, and it's easy for a

flood of guilt feelings to take over and destroy your family's chance for quality time together.

4. *Finally, play the "What would happen if" game.* This is a way to discover the best alternatives for your family. For example, what would happen if you quit work? What would happen if you only worked part time, or said, "No overtime"? What would happen if you went back to school? What would happen if you decided to change jobs? To play the game fairly you must remain open to a wide range of possible answers to each question you might pose. Don't kill this game in its prime and say, "What would happen if I quit work? Well, we would all starve!" Speculate on possible changes you could make in your life. You may find a whole new exciting life waiting for you.

Bruce Bogan and his wife did just this. Bruce was an aeronautics engineer; his wife was an artist. They felt guilty about rearing their children in the rat race of a large city. They began to ask the question "What would happen if we gave up our city jobs and moved to the country?" The move might be more conducive to an artist's career, but what would an aeronautics engineer do? They decided to make the move, and Bruce applied his engineering expertise to sculpturing. His success exceeded his wildest expectations. But the real benefit was more quality time together with the family and no more guilt.

Playing the "What would happen if" game makes you realize you do have a choice about how you are going to live your life. When you feel that you have no options or choices, then you are ripe for a heavy load of guilt, and you will find yourself relentlessly pushed down the path of least resistance.

The Problem of Illness and Fatigue

I believe in Bible promises. And as a mother, here are two promises I claim quite often.

"And ye shall serve the Lord your God . . . and I will take sickness away from the midst of thee." Exodus 23:25.

"But they that wait upon the Lord shall renew their strength; they shall mount up with wings as eagles; they shall run, and not be weary; and they shall walk, and not faint." Isaiah 40:31.

I'm glad the Lord has promised renewed health and energy, but I can't expect miracles unless I do my share and make sure my family's life style is a healthy one.

Most parents don't consider the possibility of fatigue and illness, whether their own or their child's, when they plan their life with children. Stark reality is expressed vividly by Jayme Curley, a working mother who wrote in her diary, "Shana has caught the cold I have just recovered from. David and I were up six times with her last night; she was sweaty and coughing. Of the 203 days of her life, she has been sick fifty days with colds, two with stomachaches. I've been sick seventy-four days with colds and the breast infections. David, fifteen days with colds. What a mess we've been."[1]

How do prime-time parents cope with illness and fatigue? Prevention is the best answer. As one mother told me, "I don't have time to be sick, so I put all my effort into prevention." It is also important to be realistic about our body needs and the effect that pregnancy, the post-partum period, and aging will have on our fatigue level and our general state of well-being. We must also plan realistically to deal with our children's illnesses.

Prevention

There are three general principles to follow to prevent illness and fatigue.

1. Keep your family in good physical condition by getting regular checkups at least once a year. If you have a minor problem, have it taken care of immediately. Don't allow it to develop into a difficulty.

2. Maintain good eating habits, drink plenty of water, and don't indulge in harmful practices such as drinking alcohol, taking drugs, or smoking.

3. Use your body carefully. Get plenty of rest and regular exercise (the kind that strengthens the heart muscle and lowers the heart rate). Do not abuse yourself with inactivity or drive yourself too hard.

Health habits are established early in life, so by the time you need to present a good example to your children, your own poor health habits may be deeply ingrained. But change is possible. And change may be necessary if you want to solve the problem of illness and fatigue. Belloc and Bresslow[2] found that the people who observed all of the following health practices were healthier and lived longer than those only observing a portion of these habits.

1. Usually sleep seven or eight hours.

2. Eat breakfast almost every day.
3. Eat between meals once in a while, rarely, or never.
4. Maintain a desirable weight.
5. Engage in active sports, swim, do physical exercises, or take long walks, or garden.
6. Avoid drinking.
7. Never smoke.

In addition to following these specific health habits, here are some further tips.

Coping With Fatigue

If fatigue is your problem, be sure to get enough sleep each night and take a few catnaps during the day. Find a place where you can nap during your break time. When you return home, take a fifteen-minute nap before settling into the evening routine. Perhaps the baby-sitter can stay a little longer to give you this necessary rest period, or you might ask your spouse to take over for a while.

Exercise is a good way to get rid of fatigue. Get up for five minutes every hour and move around briskly enough to feel your heart pump a little harder. Try a number of exercises to stretch and move each part of your body. If your office building has stairs, use them. If the lounge has space to jump rope—jump. If there is a recreational facility at your place of employment or nearby, use the swimming pool, racquetball or volleyball courts, or the gym.

Donna Kenmore, a reporter for a local newspaper, solved her fatigue problem when she discovered running. Now up at 6:00 a.m., her goal is to put in five miles before breakfast. Running has not only brought her increased energy, but also social experiences. She runs and socializes at the same time with her neighbor. Often her 8-year-old daughter joins her. Meeting the challenge of a competitive race has become an ego-building experience for both mother and daughter and has brought them closer together.

Diet not only affects your general health but it can also affect your level of fatigue. Diets that are high in sugars, starches, and fats have a way of slowing down the system. Eat a balanced diet with plenty of energy foods, such as vegetables and good protein. Avoid fad diets and concentrate on eating a good variety of simple, natural foods.

The amount of water you drink may affect your fatigue level, because wastes that accumulate in your body create fatigue.

The way you feel relates directly to how you act. When your body is run down, when you are tired, when your head aches, it doesn't take very much pressure to push your emotional temperature to the breaking point, and coping with the children and the job becomes an unbearable task.

Special Situations

Pregnancy, postpartum adjustment, breast-feeding, and early infant development are sometimes difficult periods for the prime-time parent. Some women continue working without difficulty. Others find the combination almost impossible. The stories of Jean, Sally, and Joyce illustrate some of the problems that can arise during this time.

Jean had never been sick a day in her life. She was a perfect specimen of physical fitness—and then she got pregnant. During the first three months she was so sick that she couldn't even hold down water and had to spend a couple of weeks in the hospital. She existed through the fourth and fifth month, but by the sixth month she was hospitalized again, and fluctuated between her bed and the hospital doors until she delivered.

Sally sailed through her pregnancy with flying colors. Her first child was born after only five hours of labor, so she was looking forward to another easy delivery—since everybody told her the second one would be even easier! It turned out that after hours of labor, the baby was breech and she was rushed to surgery for a Caesarian section. Then a slight bladder infection turned into a major kidney infection and her temperature zoomed. A simple birth turned into a life-and-death struggle. Finally, after fourteen days in the hospital, Sally went home to the demands of two little girls—a 2-year-old who couldn't understand why the family needed another little girl when she was still in good condition, and a tiny baby. Returning to work in the near future was not possible until Sally regained her strength and dealt with the demands of her family.

Joyce had a different experience. She worked right up until the day Timmy was born, and was back on her own feet within a day or two. "I'll be back to my old routine in two weeks," she told her friends at work. But little Timmy changed all that. Within four days he developed jaundice and went back to the hospital. Joyce caught a cold and had to give up breast-feeding temporarily. After three weeks she tried breast-feeding again, but little Timmy continued to have difficulties, and it was a continuous round of doctor's appointments, medications, and hospital visits for the next eight months. How could she, during this critical time, give her tender child over to some other caregiver? Her two-week vacation leave to have the baby was extended for a year until life began to smooth out and Timmy seemed stronger.

Many women are surprised by the exhaustion they feel during their pregnancy and the first few years of child rearing. The changes that occur in a woman's body during the first three months of pregnancy cause her to feel especially tired. Then, because the body is pushed out of shape and it is more difficult to get around with the extra load, a woman tires more easily as she nears the final months—the last stretch. Labor is tremendously hard work, as its name implies, and most women need a week or two (or more) before they regain their strength.

Breast-feeding can be a real joy and an extra benefit to the baby, but it does cause fatigue, and it can have some handicaps for the working mother. (Someone once told me that breast-feeding a child was as tiring as working eight hours a day. Can you imagine how tired a woman will feel if she tries to do both without getting an adequate amount of rest?) If it is necessary to be away from the baby eight to ten hours a day, then breast-feeding is difficult. But many mothers work part-time or come home for lunch and continue breast-feeding their infant. The baby receives formula supplements or bottled breast milk when Mother is not around. This system has its drawbacks when Mother comes rushing home from work to find the baby full of formula and sound asleep. She is then faced with the problem of painfully full breasts, which will probably need pumping. Other mothers routinely pump their breasts to maintain a supply for emergencies.

The second handicap for mothers who breast-feed is that when Mother is home no one else can do the feeding. For the first six months or so, Mother will be awakened two or sometimes three times per night to feed her little one. Jan helped me through this time by awakening at the first sound of a cry, changing the messy diaper, and bringing our baby to bed for me to nurse. When the baby had finished, Jan dutifully got up again and carried him back to his own bed. But not every father is a light sleeper! As long as your infant continues to wake you during the night, you are going to need extra rest during the day to make up for these interruptions.

Breast-feeding is ideal, but you need to be realistic about the difficulties that might occur, especially during the first month. Keep the local La Leche League number close at hand and don't be afraid to call for help if you need it. If job demands or other problems make breast-feeding impossible, consider the blessing of being able to share the feeding responsibility with your husband, or your baby-sitter. Remember, they too can benefit from the closeness of the feeding relationship.

When Your Child Becomes Ill

A child's illness presents a special problem to the prime-time parent who does not have a full-time caregiver at home. Here are the options that are usually available when illness strikes.

1. *Stay home.* If possible, try to stay home with a sick child. If a child is too sick or contagious to go to school or to a baby-sitter's house, then the child usually enjoys the comfort of his own bed and the warm security of his own parents meeting his needs. This can be a prime time to enjoy your child alone, without the interference of the rest of the family. Both you and your child can benefit by this closeness.

Ask your employer about the possibility of using sick-leave benefits when your child is ill. It may be possible for you to stay home part of the day and let your spouse take over for the other half. You could also hire someone to come into your home and baby-sit your sick child.

If the child's illness is not contagious or serious, then one of the following plans might be suitable:

2. *Take the sick child to work with you.* This is possible

only in certain work situations. You must consider the age of the child and the nature of the illness. When it is possible it can have advantages. You can still do your job (although your efficiency may be somewhat diminished), and you and your child are together. One day when Kim was 4 and did not feel like going to nursery school, I took her to my university class with me. It turned out to be a real education for her. After my lecture to students sitting in nice, neat rows, she said, "Mommy, I didn't know that is how you taught. I thought you sat on a little chair and all the students sat on the floor." Her concept of a teacher was obviously colored by her nursery school experience.

3. *Ask a friend to baby-sit.* Sometimes a friend who has young children or children in school might be willing to come to your home for the day and watch your sick child. If the illness isn't contagious, the sick child can be taken to your friend's home. This solution is fine if your friend is available when you need her. Think ahead about who you might call in case of an emergency.

4. *Send the child to school.* If the illness isn't contagious and the child just has an early morning slump that may be remedied as soon as he sees his friends, send him off to school. If the illness is contagious or the child is too ill to get anything out of school, then you must make other arrangements. If staying home alone with Mom becomes too special, children can retreat from normal pressures of school and act sick in order to get their parent's full attention. This situation should be avoided.

Some day-care centers have a special isolation room for children who are sick. But even without this convenience, most children can return to a child-care facility even if they are still plagued by a runny nose and an occasional cough because the contagious part of a cold is usually during the first three or four days. Most centers require a doctor's permit if there is a question about contagion.

5. *Staying home alone.* Some older children enjoy the independence and responsibility of staying home alone for a part or even a whole day. Parents should be available by phone and should call to check on the child throughout the day. If possible, a neighbor should be alerted to the situation and asked to check on the sick child occasionally. Be sure a list of emergency numbers is available. Choose this option only if your child feels good about it and you feel he can be trusted. The seriousness of the illness must be assessed before this decision is made. The length of your absence is also important. Four hours may not be too long, but ten hours may.

These suggestions may help you to plan realistically for future illness. Planning ahead will help a parent cope more effectively with a child's unexpected illness.

Turning the "Terrible" Into the "Terrific"

Every morning, rain or shine, snow or gale, Mom would greet five-year-old Jim with, "It's going to be a terrific day!" And together they would go out in the pre-dawn chill to feed the chickens and milk the cows.

"Terrific day?" With frost-bitten toes, rain soaked jacket and wind whistling in his ears, it didn't always seem terrific.

One morning Jim decided to challenge his mother's greeting. "No," he shook his head, glancing out at the threatening sky, "It's not going to be a terrific day!"

"It's not?" she questioned in a startled voice.

"No, it's not. It's going to be a terrible day!"

"Well," she replied, "If you think it's going to be a terrible day, it's going to be. You better get back into bed."

Sighing a sigh of relief, Jim pulled the warm feather tick about his neck and dozed for an hour or so until he heard the clanking of pans and smelled the inviting aroma of warm fresh bread, signaling the preparation of breakfast.

He waited an extra ten minutes to make sure he'd miss his usual breakfast time chores, then quickly dressed and headed down stairs.

"What are you doing here?" she asked in surprise.

"I'm hungry. I came for breakfast!"

"But I thought you said it was going to be a terrible day. Eating breakfast would make it terrific. You had better go back to bed." And without another word she firmly ushered him to his room.

An attempt to get lunch was met with the same action. He begged for dinner, but Mother was insistent, "You said it was going to be a terrible day—and it is. You've got to work to make a day terrific. Terrific days are terrific only if you make them terrific!"

Well said. Too many people go through life blaming others for their misery, bitter that life hasn't given them their fair share, wishing for the riches of a tomorrow that never comes. They live one terrible day after another not realizing that they have the power to turn the terrible into the terrific.

The truth is, happiness is in the heart. You can decide to be happy, no matter what the circumstances. Next time you're tempted to complain about the "terrible," remember Paul and Silas in prison. They sang. And later Paul, from a deep dark dungeon in Rome, wrote, "Rejoice in the Lord always: and again I say, Rejoice." (Philippians 4:4.) If anyone had reason to complain or bemoan their plight these men had!

One day a woman complained that her husband always treated her like a child. He made all the decisions.

"Well," her friend replied, "Does he make bad decisions?"

"No."

"Does he squander the money?"

"No."

"Does he carouse and come home drunk?"

"No."

"Does he forbid you from going to church?"

"No."

"Well then, you have the best of the worst! It seems to me that you have a lot more to be thankful for than to complain about!"

And what does all this have to do with God's kids? Just this: Children reflect their parents' moods. If you can have a "terrific" day even though everything goes wrong, your child can too. Learn to say, "Thank you God" for everything that comes your way. Notice the little blessings. Dwell on God's answers to your prayers. When troublous times come, smile and say, "OK God, what do You want me to learn from this? Help me find a spark of positive in this mess!"

And God can. He stilled the wind and waves. Why can't He send a ray of sun through your gloom?

Next time your child puckers up her little face or your son whines for his dinner, check yourself. When was the last time they heard you sing a happy song? When last did your voice reflect the excitement of living? When last did you compliment your child or comment about the blessings God is showering upon you? When was the last time you smiled and said, "It's going to be a terrific day!"

Banish the negative and soak in the positive. Follow this advice: "Finally, brethren (parents), whatsoever things are true, whatsoever things are honest, whatsoever things are just, whatsoever things are pure, whatsoever things are of good report; if there be any virtue, and if there be any praise, think on these things." (Philippians 4:8.)

Chances are you have far more to be happy and thankful for than to be downcast about. Smile and enjoy the happy reflection of your child.

Make Your Family a Winning Team

I love being on a winning team. That's one reason I'm a Christian. With Jesus as my coach (my Creator and Redeemer) I'll never lose! His team is going through to the kingdom.

But God doesn't want just me—He wants my family, too. I know He'll ask someday, "Kay, where is the flock that was given thee, thy beautiful flock?" (Jeremiah 13:20), and I'll want to answer, "Right here, Lord." I want everyone in my family to be a winner.

A superstar is not the key to a winning team—either in sports or in the family. You, the parent, have the ability to mold an aggregation of individuals with different interests, goals, personalities, and needs into a body that functions as one.

"There should be no schism (division) in the body; but that the members should have the same care one for another. And whether one member suffer, all the members suffer with it; or one member be honored, all the members rejoice with it." 1 Corinthians 12:25, 26.

A winning team is a group of people who believe that team glory is more important than individual glory. They will not jeopardize the team in order to make a name for themselves. Each member of the family must feel vitally important and essential, *but the family must come first.* This is not a popular philosophy in a society that believes the most important thing is to look out for yourself. But it is a winning-team philosophy.

For example: How did the Boston Celtics achieve the outstanding record of winning the National Basketball Association Championship eleven times out of thirteen? They were not a rich team, they did not have the fans (Boston's big winter sport is hockey), nor did they then have the superstars (no Celtic ever led the league in scoring). The Celtics became a winning team primarily because Red Auerbach, their coach, insisted that the team was more important than a superstar. He knew how to mold team effort and team spirit so the team as a whole became greater than the sum of its parts.

As the spirit of a basketball, baseball, or football team and its morale are closely linked, so are the spirit and morale of the family team. And you can protect this spirit in several ways. Encourage each family member to understand his own importance and the primary importance of the family. Make sure that every family member feels needed. Establish a buddy system in which each person is responsible for another. Finally, inspire your children to conduct themselves as champions.

Superstars seldom make it to the top by themselves. In team sports, the outstanding player owes much of his success to the support of his teammates, just as every individual in one way or another owes much of his success to his family.

The superstar of a family might be a parent who is a famous scientist, or an outstanding musician, or president of a company. It may be a child who is a born athlete or intellectually gifted. If these individuals overshadow other family members or receive attention and recognition at the others' expense, there will be a breakdown in family morale. Each superstar must learn to accept recognition graciously, and honestly credit the family when credit is due.

Children who are not superstars sometimes feel neglected, worthless, and unloved because they do not receive the attention that another is receiving. The family cannot always prevent this if the attention comes from outsiders. But within the family they can make sure that all of their children receive recognition for their skills and abilities, even if the outside world has not crowned that child with superstar status. Each team member should be challenged to do his best; and when he does, superstar status should be granted by the family!

Even with precautions, though, family members may be overshadowed by the family superstar at times. When one member of the family has achieved status and recognition, it's easy for the rest of the family to be known as so-and-so's wife, husband, son, brother, or sister. These individuals may find it difficult to establish their own identity because they can never hope to match or surpass the superstar.

In such cases, parents must make it very clear that striving to become a superstar is not necessary. Children do not have to match or exceed another sibling's accomplishments. They must simply try to do their best at all times. The scope of your achievements is less important than the spirit with which you tackle them. Borrow a phrase from Winston Churchill as your family motto: "Success is never final. Failure is never fatal. It's courage that counts."

Neither children nor other family members should feel

that the family must revolve around them—that they are the center of their universe and that their wants, wishes, and needs will always preempt everyone else's.

One woman told me a sad story of her own childhood: "I saw my mother give *everything* to her girls. Dad was excluded altogether too much. I got smothered. Dad was starved. I would have liked to see my parents enjoy each other more in such things as play, sports, entertainment, and friends.

"I came to marriage unequipped to have fun with my husband. Unless a child can receive a warm, happy feeling from seeing his or her parents enjoy themselves together with and without him, he may be crippled for adulthood."

Children must realize that parents have needs too—that Mom and Dad need time alone, that appointments must be met, that out-of-town travel is sometimes necessary, and that business crises do arise that require time away from the family. If a family has a team spirit, these occasional inconveniences can be viewed as opportunities rather than handicaps. For example, when Mom is sick, Junior won't feel cheated because no one has prepared his dinner. Instead, he can turn the situation into a challenge and prepare the family meal.

A winning team cannot function effectively when one or two members always get their way at the expense of others. It destroys the team spirit of those who are neglected.

In my opinion, the breakdown of the family in today's society is primarily a result of losing a team spirit. Too many people have the mistaken sense that "I can do it by myself," or "With enough self-assertiveness I can make it to the top without anyone else." When one has this attitude, there is little need for a family. The family only hampers progress because it demands time and attention. Too often, children are pushed into the background by parents who don't realize the importance of a family team.

Do it together. December 7, 1979, is a day our family will never forget. After a year and a half of tiptoeing past the study door, the family project, *Prime-Time Parenting,* was finished and sent off to Rawson, Wade Publishers in New York. To celebrate, we ordered "WE DID IT" T-shirts.

Was it really a family project? Yes, from start to finish. The suggestions in the book came from living with three active, creative children. Jan spent extra time fathering. And they all carried more than their share of home responsibilities while pretending Mommy was in Africa. Kim, Kari, and Kevin continually prayed for "Mommy's book," and rejoiced with each finished chapter. Why not celebrate this family accomplishment? The first night after wearing our shirts Kevin prayed, "Dear Jesus, please help us to have fun with our 'WE DID IT' shirts." His prayer has been answered!

Sometimes parents do find themselves overextended—pushing for deadlines over which they have little control. Rather than detracting from the family and letting these pressures destroy your chance of playing on a winning team, why not involve the family? Let them feel they are an important part of the project. And then celebrate when it is over and give everyone a superstar award.

To build an effective team, every member must feel that he can contribute to the overall team goal or purpose. In this way, every family member can feel important—a superstar on a winning team.

Loyalty to the Family

"Yuk, brothers are bratty. I wish mine were dead." "You ought to have a bossy sister like I have. She drives me up a wall!"

Why is it that the "in" thing to do is to down-grade family members, especially siblings, in front of your friends? Perhaps it makes the insecure child feel superior by belittling others. Perhaps they think that since others do it, to be accepted they have to participate in this type of down-grading, too. Perhaps because loyalty to peers is so strong during these years, they have to prove this loyalty by being disloyal to their family.

Whatever the reason, I believe the disloyal attitude toward a family member even if indulged in sporatically to get a laugh from the crowd, is damaging to family relationships. Parents should know that this demeaning talk is engaged in by the vast majority of school children and take active steps to teach their children the importance of family loyalty.

1. Establish the principle, "I'm my brother's keeper," as family policy. You are each responsible for the other.

2. Start a buddy system where each person has a family

member he looks out for in a special way, not allowing anyone else to hurt him. Change each week so each one has an opportunity to look out for each of the others.

3. Explain the family team concept. Don't down-grade your own teammates to the opposition. Stick up for your own. Pick them up when they are down. When one has a problem, gather around. Support each other in the time of need.

4. Stop demeaning talk within the household. Arguments may arise but words and actions meant to hurt another must never be used.

5. Don't talk negatively about anyone else including those in the church or school family.

6. Treat your spouse and children with respect. Don't discuss their faults with others.

7. If the children are caught demeaning another, they should have to tell two nice things about that person for every negative comment.

8. Role play how to answer when a peer starts saying nasty things about their own sibling—or about yours.

9. Engage in a little T.A. (transactional analysis). When someone down-grades another they are speaking in their parent personality. The way you shrink their "parent" is to give them three warm fuzzies. It works. Try it.

10. Encourage the family to do nice things for each other. Once a month have a "car wash" day where you "wash" the selected family member all day with compliments and warm fuzzies. On the day of the month that is your child's birthday date, have that be the child's special day where you surprise him with kindness in some way. Twelve times a year isn't too often to get this type of special treatment.

11. Do things together. If one member has a recital,

everybody be willing to go to support, encourage, and compliment that person.

12. Teach every child to be quick to give credit to other family members for helping in their own success. The idea that a successful person gets there alone is not true. Give the family the credit when credit is due.

13. Loyalty to friends is high during the school-age years. Discuss how the children would feel if their friend said mean things about them behind their backs. Relate this to the family showing family members feel the same way.

14. When mistakes are made, don't get in the habit of blaming others. Look for the reasons why a family member erred rather than criticizing that person for his stupidity.

15. Read Romans 12:10, "Be kindly affectioned one to another with brotherly love," and discuss with the family what the Lord is saying to your family in this text.

Learning to be loyal to your family is the first step in learning to be loyal to other segments of society and to God. Let's stick up for each other. We'll all feel stronger and more secure knowing we have the support of a loyal family behind us—a group of people who always see us in the best possible light.

Step-Parenting Success

Did you have the idea that blending your one parent family with another was going to be the fulfillment of your dreams for an ideal family? His, hers, and ours living together happily ever after. You were disillusioned, weren't you?

Being a step-parent isn't easy. Step parents experience more anxiety, anger, and depression than biological parents. And the hardest job seems to be step-parenting older children. Here is why and what you can do about it.

Many children of divorce continue to fantasize that their parents may someday get back together. A remarriage bursts this bubble of hope and they resent the step parent's intrusion. Solve the problems of the past before your new marriage. Start by talking about the past divorce and about the children's desire that their parents might someday live together again. By having these things out in the open, by venting pent-up feelings, the child has emotional space to begin dealing with current problems. When it is clear that a new marriage is to take place, talk to your children about how other children have felt living with step-parents and how they, too, are likely to have these feelings.

Children may want their parent to remarry but during

the single period they enjoyed having their parent's exclusive time and attention—sometimes even sleeping in the parent's bed. When a remarriage occurs the new spouse usurps this special role, making the child feel left out and unnecessary. To avoid this, talk to your child frankly. "We've been very close since I haven't been married. However, if my new marriage is to be as God wants it to be, my spouse and I will have to become so close we'll be like one person—the Bible says one flesh. Marriage is a unique relationship; different from the parent-child relationship, but you may not understand this until you someday are married. When I marry, you may at times feel left out. I don't want this to happen. Even though I love my spouse, it will in no way change my love for you. I want you to always feel loved and wanted. So tell us when you feel neglected so we can do whatever necessary to change your feelings. It will be easy for you to pout and say, 'If they don't need me, I don't need them.' Many children choose this route. But in the long run it won't make you happy. We need each other. But we've got to be able to talk hurts over if we want to solve them and grow in this new family relationship."

Children may want a new dad or mom but they may not be thrilled with the idea of having to share their own parent, toys, and home space with stepbrothers and sisters. Make sure each child has things of his own. He should have the choice whether or not to share. You want a cheerful giver—not a reluctant one. The more you love someone the more you want to share. Don't force decisions upon a child such as a new brother or sister moving into his room. Let him come up with the idea. Plan so your child has abundant time with you alone. Don't needlessly incite jealousy by flaunting your attention on the stepfamily in the presence of your child. Don't make your own child a scapegoat as you are trying to win the love of a step child. Even out words of correction. Be fair to all.

"Don't tell me what to do. You're not my daddy," is a common cry of stepchildren. A child resents anyone's discipline if it's not balanced with love and affection. In the step relationship, the focus of the first couple years should be convincing the child of your love. Avoid restrictive discipline. Use natural or logical consequences so the child can see the justice of your actions. Let the child have a choice by negotiating contracts or allowing him to choose his punishment. Make sure you and your spouse agree on discipline. Otherwise, children capitalize on the situation. They don't have to take lessons on how to divide and conquer!

Teenagers often feel a lack of privacy as strangers of the opposite sex move into the house. Some fear sexual harassment. You may need to encourage modesty. Perhaps policies about time limits for bathroom use could be established. Locks on bedroom doors may relieve anxiety. If a child fears being left alone with new family members of the opposite sex, respect that fear. Don't be blind to potential problems. Your child may be the best judge of the situation. A good healthy love relationship will eventually dispell the fear. If not, counseling may be helpful.

Children are often frustrated by a divided sense of loyalty. "I can't love my stepmother because that might make my own mother angry and jealous and she would stop loving me." You can diminish the chances of this happening by making sure satisfactory custody and visiting rights are established before entering a new relationship. If biological parents are still punishing each other by using the children as pawns, this increases the children's confusion about their loyalties. Don't make loyalty an issue by asking for loyalty pledges. Say positive things about the child's other parent. Encourage the child to talk about his feelings of mixed loyalty. Let him know your love for him is not dependent on his choosing you or the other parent. You'll love him no matter what choices he makes.

Children sometimes compare the stepparent to their biological parent. Stepparents seldom win such contests. "My real mother never did it that way." "If my real father knew how you're treating me, he'd let you have it." "You don't belong here; this is our house, not yours."

It's hard not to defend yourself when the barbs fly. But if you do, you'll probably end up in deeper water. Your best defense is to listen to the *feelings* behind the words. Show you understand those feelings by making comments such as, "It's hard to have another man move into the house where your daddy once lived." "You really feel angry when you don't have your daddy to yourself anymore and must share him with me, a stranger."

Then after you've listened, you may want to send an "I feel" statement of your own: "I feel hurt when you accuse me of unkind things because I need and want your friendship."

Finally, when you feel the "enemy" is gaining ground and you're beginning to wonder how you ever got yourself into this mess, retreat to a quiet place and read Psalm 37 over and over again. You'll feel better—I know you will.

Even though step-parenting may not be easy, you can find satisfaction by facing squarely the problems and focusing on the benefits.

Grandparenting

The Bible credits a Godly mother and grandmother as the ones primarily responsible for instilling a love of God in the boy Timothy. (2 Timothy 1:5.) Wouldn't you like to have that kind of influence on your grandchildren?

Grandparents are a blessing every child should enjoy. They may not spend much time with the child, but their example and instruction will be remembered for a lifetime. That's why it is so important that parents and grandparents love and respect each other.

Conflict between parents and grandparents can be devastating to children. Add a divorce and remarriage with the resulting extra sets of grandparents and the complexity of relationships can be mind-boggling. Mutual respect is essential if the child is to survive unscathed. Each parent and grandparent is an authority figure to the child. When something is said about the other that lowers the child's respect for either their parent's or grandparent's authority, it diminishes that person's effectiveness.

Grandparents, your primary role is to give the child time and attention—a little extra love to cushion the bumps and bruises in life. Encourage the child to see the positive. Give him a sense of optimism; hope. Surprise him with kindness. Do the little extra things that bring a sparkle to his eyes and lilt to his step. You don't have to live next door to fulfill this role. A letter with a piece of sugarless gum has given, loud and clear, the "I love you" message to my children.

Discipline? Yes, I believe all adults should take the responsibility of correcting children and teaching them appropriate behavior. But don't go overboard. If you question how much disciplining you should be doing, ask the parents. They would rather be asked than have to bring up the subject themselves if they think you are too strict or too permissive in your relationship with the children. I don't believe grandparents (or parents either) should be harsh and unreasonable, meting out painful punishment. I have found that when children have a special love relationship with their grandparents, the need for discipline is usually diminished.

The third aspect of the grandparenting role is showing respect to the child's parents—even when you don't agree or when you did things differently yourself as a parent.

I know a lot of parents aren't the kind of parents grandparents want for their grandchildren. But showing disapproval of the parent's behavior in front of the child, or talking with a child about that parent behind his back will only make matters worse. If at all possible the grandparent must uphold the parent's action to the child, sometimes explaining, "Your daddy spanked you because he told you three times to be quiet and you didn't pay any attention. You must be careful not to make your daddy angry." If you feel the action was too severe (or lenient), talk to the parent in private, don't undermine. Only when physical or psychological child abuse occurs should grandparents (or others) interfere.

Respect the parent's right to establish routines and health habits for their children. If parents say no inbetween snacks, don't tempt little ones with your nibbling; if sweets are banned, don't slip jelly beans to the kids on the sly. If bedtime is at nine o'clock, don't let Junior watch the late show. Parents will appreciate your support and the children will benefit from a united front.

Many parents today have chosen different methods of discipline from those you may be familiar with. Be willing to accept these differences. Parents need encouragement, not criticism.

You can be a great grandparent by appropriately loving and disciplining your grandchildren. But your acceptance and respect for your own child or son or daughter in-law as parents is the most important factor in assuring a minimum of conflict between the generations and a maximum of pleasure.

Keep Their Love Cups Full

Children need lots of loving! Psalm 23 says that God keeps our cups so full they overflow. That's the way children's cups should be.

Children cannot live without love. Many years ago in a study of orphans in Tehran, it was found that after a year or two some children were not sitting up or walking, and many died. Why? They had enough food, each one had a crib, and their diapers were changed regularly. Didn't they have everything they needed? No, the essential ingredient for growth was missing. No one touched, cuddled or rocked them. Nobody loved them. Their love cups did not overflow. They were empty.

Without attention, children don't feel loved. So if their love cups are empty, they try to get them filled with attention. They seek approval, they show off, they try to be good. But how often do good children get much attention? Not often. Most unloved children find they get more attention by being bad. Getting attention becomes such an overwhelming need that these children cease to care if it is positive or negative. Being yelled at or beaten is better than being ignored.

How can we make sure our children receive the love they

need to be loving individuals? First of all, avoid emptying your child's love cup. Here are some of the most common ways to make your child feel unloved: (1) by showing approval only when the child is good; (2) by ridiculing the child in an attempt to correct him; (3) by threatening the child; (4) by expressing a critical attitude; (5) by screaming at the child; (6) by expressing disappointment or disgust by sighing; (7) by giving the child the silent treatment; (8) by being too busy; (9) by breaking love routines; (10) by using the child's name negatively.

We must concentrate on filling our children's love cups. The most important way is by *accepting* each child just the way he is. Let him know that he is always wanted and welcome. Try to understand his behavior. If we think about behavior as being caused, and not just inherent in the child, then we can look beyond the immediate behavior to what's causing it and still be loving to our children. Let's respect them.

The second thing is to *listen carefully* to each child. We need to create a comfortable and warm atmosphere where he feels free to express himself. As we listen, let's react with sensitivity and meet his needs.

Finally, we must *spend time* with each child. Cuddle, hold, hug, and touch when it's appropriate. Let each child know you enjoy being with him and are always willing to meet his needs. Spending time caring for his physical and emotional needs is much more important than giving things to the child.

Now, try this experiment. When your child is being particularly difficult and unloving, instead of giving him your usual cup-emptying treatment, try filling his cup instead. Show that you can accept him even though you don't approve of his actions. Treat him with respect. Listen carefully to the message his words and actions are trying to get across, then spend a little extra time together with him. You'll be surprised how effective this treatment can be for turning unloving children into lovable ones.

Keep your child's love cup full. Then just as we can say, "Because the Lord is my shepherd I have everything I need," your child can say, "Because Mom and Dad are my parents, I have everything I need. My cup overflows."

The Overflowing Cup

"Thou preparest a table before me
in the presence of my enemies;
thou anointest my head with oil,
my cup overflows.
Surely goodness and mercy
shall follow me
all the days of my life;
and I shall dwell in the house
of the Lord for ever."
—*Psalm 23:5, 6, RSV.*

Love Unconditionally

A child once asked his mother, "Why do you love me?"

"Why do you think?" responded his mother.

"I don't know," replied the child. "How can you really love me when I'm so naughty sometimes?"

"I don't like some of the things you do," she said, "but that doesn't mean I stop loving you when you're bad. I love you all the time."

"But why?" the little one insisted.

"Try again," encouraged Mommy. "Why do you think I love you?"

"I know," the child said. "You love me because sometimes I'm good. I do exactly what you say; I make my bed and comb my hair and eat my vegetables and—That's why you love me."

"It's very nice when you're so good, but I love you all the time."

"Why?" queried the child.

"Because," replied his mommy, "you're my child. That's why. From the moment I first saw you I loved you. I love you all the time, because you are mine."

"Wow!" said the child. "I'm glad you love me all the

time. I'm glad mommies and daddies are like that."[1]

But are mommies and daddies like that? Do they really love their children all the time? Or is their love conditional on the child's behavior—giving love when the child is good and withdrawing it when he's bad?

A study that was done at a religious university found that many students felt hostile toward the school and toward the church that sponsored it. Why this hostility toward authority? As the data were analyzed, one significant difference was found between the hostile and non-hostile students. It was the way the students felt they were loved by their parents. The hostile students felt their parents loved them conditionally—only when they were good. The others felt their parents loved them all the time, no matter what they did.[2]

Most children who feel loved conditionally don't go around intentionally saying and doing things to make their parents angry. They want to be loved, so they try extra hard to be good, even if that means bottling up their negative emotions. This is probably what had happened with those hostile students. During their growing years they didn't talk about their negative feelings toward their parents when minor misunderstandings occurred, but kept these feelings inside, fearing that if they told their parents, their parents wouldn't love them. Later, they transferred their hostility to safer authority figures—the school and the church.

Can you see the ultimate result of this transference of hostility? Parental love is to the child a model of God's love. If parents love conditionally, children reason that God must too. If hostility toward authority continues to grow, it can affect the child's relationship to God, the ultimate authority!

In addition, conditional love is deadly to a child's sense

of self-worth. If you're not loved for who you are, you must not be very valuable. If you want to be loved (and who doesn't?), you must always change to fit what others want you to be; you must always say what others want you to say. You become afraid to make decisions. What if you make a mistake? Will you be rejected? It's so much safer to let someone else make decisions for you. You become dependent, insecure, unsure of yourself.

But do parents really love their children conditionally? If I were to go back and ask the parents in the study if they loved their children only when they were good, I am sure most of them would say, "No. Of course not!" But, you see, how they love is not so important as how the child perceives he is loved. It is the message that comes through to the child that is so important. Saying, "I love you all the time," and acting loving only when the child is good confuses the child into feeling loved conditionally.

So if you want your child to feel accepting toward authority, to be able to make decisions, and to feel good about himself, you must make sure you deliver the message of unconditional love. Say it loud and clear with your words and actions. "I love you all the time because you are mine." That's how parents must love!

That's how parents must love—because that's how God loves His children. This is what Paul said about God's love, "For I am persuaded, that neither death, nor life, nor angels, nor principalities, nor powers, nor things present, nor things to come, Nor height, nor depth, nor any other creature, shall be able to separate us from the love of God, which is in Christ Jesus our Lord." (Romans 8:38, 39.)

Helping Children Love And Respect Authority

"And now, Israel, what doth the Lord thy God require of thee, but to fear (respect) the Lord thy God, to walk in all his ways, and to love him, and to serve the Lord thy God with all thy heart and with all thy soul." (Deuteronomy 10:12.)

If this is what the Lord requires of His people, then parents have a responsibility to help children learn to love and respect their heavenly Father.

Learning to love and respect authority is the foundation for spiritual development. God is our heavenly parent—and our supreme authority. How a child views God's authority will be colored by his attitude toward you, his parents.

A child can either live in fear of authority figures or he can love and respect them. Authorities come in two extremes. The judge, policeman, justice-demanding authority (the type I fear when I accidentally go through a stop sign) or the specialist type (one who is an expert in his field). I fear the first. I love and respect the second. As a parent I much prefer being the specialist type. I want to be such an expert in my parenting career that my children will love and respect me. And I believe the specialist type of parental authority best expresses the kind of God who so loved us that He gave His Son to die for us.

But if you are not careful, you can be responsible for teaching your child to fear authority and to ultimately serve God out of fear of punishment—or to openly rebel and reject God's gift of salvation. Here is how.

Use Force. Apply the "do it or else" philosophy. Make a habit of saying, "I don't care what you think, I said to . . ." Spank the child for every misdemeanor so he has no choice but to obey.

Did you know a "good" shepherd never uses his rod to beat the sheep into submission? Instead the rod is used to block dangerous paths, to lead, to protect. Force is not a part of God's government. The devil is the one who employs this type of manipulation.

When pushed or prodded children tend to resist. Instead of applying the rod of punishment when they hesitate, take their hand, talk to them, encourage them, lead them and you'll find less defiance. When forced into submission, children tend to rebel. They may submit externally and comply to your demands, but too often it is because of fear—and their attitude toward you as an authority is, "Just wait until I'm grown up and I'll show you you can't boss me around—or I'll run away—or I'll . . ." Rejection of parental authority is the first step toward rejection of God.

Make all the rules—all 9342 of them. After all, you know best. Why waste time with the democratic process? When God gave us His ten commandments, He didn't ask us what we thought. Why shouldn't you treat your child the same?

Here's why. You're not God. You make mistakes. Some of the rules you make for your children you, at times, may bend for your own convenience. Rule 587: "No eating between meals." But you were starved. Rule 2079: "Only thirty minutes of TV per day." But the football game lasted three hours.

Parents must be responsible for good home government, but instead of thousands of parent-imposed rules that apply only to the children, try three unbendable principles that can apply to the whole household. Principle 1: You may not hurt yourself. Principle 2: You may not hurt others. Principle 3: You may not hurt things. Then let the children take part in making up more specific rules based on these three principles. For example: "No playing in the street because you can't hurt yourself." "No hitting, because you can't hurt others." "No jumping on the beds because you can't hurt things." By allowing the child to be a part of the decision-making process, you'll find more willing compliance to the rules and more of a responsibility to police himself and others.

Expect immediate and perfect obedience. When I say "jump," jump. Adults are to be obeyed. They know best. Don't ask why. Just do it.

A child's ability to obey during the preschool years is determined by whether he hears the command, is able to comprehend it, has no distractions, has the skills which make compliance possible and has the necessary motivation.

When I'm involved with a task, I dislike someone interrupting me, especially if the request could wait until I'm finished. Could children possibly feel the same way? How they must love the authority of their parents when they must jump at every beck and call; when they are given no reason why the task is necessary and must comply immediately even though it could wait until a more convenient time! Let's respect our children's need to understand the reason why we ask them to do certain things. Let's be reasonable in what and when we make requests, and they will sooner respect us.

Punish every misdemeanor. Make it painful to err. A broken rule demands retribution. Justice requires the crime be punished, and punished severely so the lesson will never be forgotten. When children live under this judicial system it makes them want to hide their mistakes. They live in fear of being discovered, and will probably lie their way out of tight situations. Plus, they feel guilty if they err and no one catches them. They are often driven to confession not because they really feel sorry for what they have done, but because they feel guilty. Often, they end up punishing themselves.

Don't forget, justice must be balanced by mercy. Accidents do happen. Being merciful and comforting a child who has erred by mistake or out of ignorance may be one of the most effective ways for a child to love and respect your authority. You could have lowered the boom. It was your right as the authority. But instead you showed understanding. A child loves and respects an authority who can be that understanding.

Keep your distance—avoid familiarity. Dictate and command. Never fraternize with subordinates. Respect is held by distance. It may work for ship captains—but not for parents.

Parents, if you want your children to love and respect your authority, be fun to live with. Play with your children, talk to them, sometimes be silly and giggle. They will love it. Get involved in their sports. Try out your rusty soccer skills or let them see that you, too, can strike out or miss a pass. Be a good model for them on how to cope with imperfection.

Parents, lead your children to love and respect your authority and you will be building their spiritual foundation of love and respect for God. It is during the preschool years when this lesson can most easily be taught. Don't miss this important opportunity.

Help Me Discipline My Children

The question, "Am I my brother's keeper?" (Genesis 4:9) has been voiced by many. Perhaps the most common situation is when children are misbehaving. "Should I, or should I not, step in and teach the child what is appropriate? Will I offend the parent? How will the child react? Perhaps I'd better just mind my own business! So the child goes uncorrected or the parent struggles alone trying to teach the child obedience.

Parents at times need help disciplining their children; they need support and encouragement, not criticism. Some day I hope it can be said of the Christian community; "They helped every one his neighbour; and every one said to his brother, Be of good courage." (Isaiah 41:6.)

All I anticipated when I stepped into the elevator on the twelfth floor was a ride to the lobby. But I got more than I asked for—a lesson that would last me a lifetime.

In the elevator I found a rather massive yet pleasant-looking gentleman. At the tenth floor the door opened, and a mother and her small son entered. It was obvious from the moment we saw them that their rapport was at a rather low ebb. As the elevator descended, their voices crescendoed!

"But why can't I have it? You promised I could have it, Mommy."

"No, I didn't promise you anything."

"You're just mean to me. You never give me anything I want."

"Hush, you know that isn't true! You're just angry!"

"I'm not either angry! I'm mad! I want it and I'm going to get it!"

"No, you're not!"

And just about the time the spiteful 4-year-old was spitting out "I hate you; you're a mean old mother," there resounded throughout the elevator chamber the massive gentleman's booming voice.

"Sonny," he ordered, "you listen to your mother!"

The mother looked up in surprised relief as we made the rest of the descent in silence. By the time we reached the lobby, the little boy had placed his hand into his mother's hand, and they peacefully walked out of our lives.

Now, I am a mother with three children, and there are times I wish I'd meet that massive gentleman again. For example, there was the time I went shopping for new carpeting, and the children discovered that the stacks of rolled-up carpet made a fascinating "jungle gym." I had no idea of the children's intentions when they asked whether they could go over to the stacks.

"OK, children," I replied, "but please walk and keep your voices down while you're in the store." By the time I looked around to check on their whereabouts, all three were at the top of the first stack and about to tackle the second.

"Come down immediately," I commanded. But they didn't! Excusing myself from the salesman who had come to serve me, I walked over to the children, and they, like most children being stalked, ran. At the command to "Stop," they halted. Explaining why they should not climb on the carpet, I marched them over to where the salesman was waiting and made them sit on the floor, ordering them to stay there until I was finished.

As I continued to talk to the salesman, my three little ones, growing restless, began pinching and tickling one another. Getting up to escape the sisterly torment, Kevin climbed once more to the top of the forbidden carpet pile. The girls eagerly reported his whereabouts.

"Kevin, get down this minute. *And I mean it!*" I responded.

I watched as he started to climb down, and then, thinking all was well, I turned back to the salesman. But Kevin not finishing the descent, there arose another outcry from his sisters.

Again saying "Excuse me" to the salesman, I went over to Kevin and lifted him from the carpet pile. Feeling I couldn't trust his 4-year-old self-control, I carried him back to the salesman and attempted to hold his squirming body while I finished getting the information I wanted.

Needless to say, by this time I was rather frustrated. My anger had risen to such a point that I was about to scream at the girls and give Kevin a good walloping. I wished my elevator friend would happen on the scene and in his booming voice command, "Sonny, you listen to your mother!"

Obviously I needed help. I needed support. I needed someone who owned the carpet to say in a firm manner, "Sonny, this carpet belongs to this store and you are not to climb on it." This simple gesture would have made my job of disciplining much easier.

Host's Cooperation Helpful

When my family visits in other people's homes, I try to keep the children on their best behavior. Sometimes my monologue runs, "Don't touch" and "Don't do that" and "Watch your feet" and "Don't be so loud" and. . . . I end up sounding like a terrible nag. Later, on a number of occasions, I have found out that the children who live in the house were doing the very things I had asked my children not to do. Sometimes a host or hostess has even said to me, "That's OK, our children do that all the time."

It would make my job much easier if only I could rely on a host to set the standards of conduct that they expect while my children are on their premises and then clearly and firmly announce this to my children. This would help me avoid making unnecessary demands on the children, and I could more fully relax and enjoy the stay if I knew that I was not totally responsible for their behavior.

Experience has taught me that when the host sets limits, it is usually much more effective than if I struggle alone to perfect the behavior of my children. Alone, I'm like the "bad guy" always "lowering the boom" and keeping them from having fun, while no one else seems to care. I'd like my children to know that other people do care and aren't afraid to say so.

I have encountered some parents who feel that when someone else corrects their children, it is a reflection on their ability as a parent, and hence a rebuke to them. If all of us (especially church members) could be more accepting of one another's child-rearing techniques and instead of criticizing other parents, help them, we might be able to *show* a more effective way of working with a child. This would probably be much less threatening to parents and more meaningful in the long run. After a few such friendly encounters, parents might learn to trust the motives of others who wish to be helpful by correcting the children when they need it.

Some parents feel that their children's feelings will be hurt if they are corrected by someone else. Older children who are seldom disciplined by anyone other than parents, teachers, or very close family friends often feel offended when correction becomes necessary. If children are disciplined and never loved by others, then I can see how this discipline might hurt their tender feelings.

Discipline should be administered in a spirit of love, and this is possible simply by stating in a caring way the reality of the situation. For example, "That tree limb looks as if it might break with so many children on it; only one at a time," rather than critically demanding, "You boys shouldn't be climbing that tree. You'll break that branch and you'll be sorry."

It is best if those who discipline children also spend time showing love and attention to them. Especially is this true after someone has had to discipline another's child. In this way a rapport is built up between adult and child. The child can learn to trust and respect a strange adult's judgment about what is appropriate behavior because he knows that person really cares for him and is not just a "grouch" or can't mind his own business.

So, if you hear my children making too much noise in church, don't tell me after church that I should keep my children quiet, but reach over right then and there, tap the noisy one on the shoulder, and with a tender smile tell him you can't hear the sermon when he is making so much noise.

If you hear one of my children say something unkind, don't tell me about it later, when it is difficult to piece together the who, what, when, and why of the situation, but kindly tell him on the spot that his words made someone unhappy and that the kind thing to do would be to apologize.

If you see my children doing something that could be harmful to themselves, others, or property, don't wait to tell me after the damage has been done, but call to them immediately and tell them gently, but firmly, they had better change their course of action, or somebody or something might get hurt.

I want my children to develop strong Christian characters. I'm trying hard to do my best to teach them appropriate ways of behaving, through my love and my discipline, but I'm not always around, or I may not always be as effective as I wish I were. When that time comes, I pray there will be someone there—someone who cares enough to help me discipline.

Three Steps to Developing God's Talents

Step 1: Discovering talent.

Remember the story of the talents? To one was given five, to another two, and another one. (Matthew 25:14-30.) But regardless of the number, the Lord expected those talents to be used and multiplied.

Each child is given special gifts from the Lord to be developed and used in His service. God created us with limitless potential. It's His desire that each one of His children is to strive for excellence, not to make a name for himself, but to do a more noble work for Him and to bless humanity.

Encouraging a child to develop his talents is an important parental task. With each new skill a child gains confidence, independence, recognition, and self-worth. A child feels good about himself when he knows he can do something well. And competence in one area has a way of encouraging the development of competence in other areas.

Whether or not a child will excel is determined by two prerequisites: A spark of natural God-given ability and a blaze of interest. Become a talent scout and help your child discover his potential. No one knows your child as well as you. What are his strong points, his natural abilities? Is he tall, robust, slight, agile? Each characteristic may open or shut certain doors. If your budding genius is 14 and nearing 6 feet, his chances of making it in basketball are good—if his interest and natural ability is there. But as for a jockey—he's out! Parents make a dreadful mistake when they impose their own interests on a child who has God-given talents in a totally different area.

You can help your child discover his talents by introducing him to the thousands of possibilities out there. When interest ignites with natural ability, the child will be motivated to do the rest.

Start with your own interests and skills. If you love great literature, introduce him to Shakespeare and Thoreau. If you're a computer bug, let her do some programming. If entimology has been your life study, take him on your next trip to collect specimens. One of the best tennis players I know started playing doubles with his Dad. Team up. You may find you and your child are a winning combination. But the chances are just as likely that his talents and interests lie in areas different from yours.

Children should be acquainted with individuals from many walks of life. When your child shows a spark of interest in a career, arrange for him to spend a few hours or a day with an individual on the job. These contacts may open up other possibilities and may lead to a life work. Ask others how they got started in their chosen field. So often they testify of the impact of becoming acquainted with an expert. For example, "I was never interested in astronomy until a man who built his own telescope let me take a peek. When I saw the rings of Saturn and the moons of Jupiter I knew what I wanted to do." "When a neighbor taught me how to train a colt, I decided working with horses was the greatest experience in the world." "On a trip to Baja, Dad arranged for a marine biologist to take me scuba diving. He cracked the mystery of the underwater world just enough to make me realize I wanted to spend the rest of my life doing the same."

Search the unusual. There may be high competition in the flute or trumpet sections of band, but what about the oboe, bassoon, or tuba? And it doesn't take a costly investment to blow a harmonica or bow away on a saw. But what a unique talent! Not every child can make it in sports, but your child may have a flair for entertaining and could pick up some magic tricks, puppetry, or ventriliquism. All these skills can be used for the Lord. Oils may not be her media, but sculpturing or whittling may capture her attention. The story is told of the young lad Antonio Stradivari in Cremona, Italy, in the middle 17th century. A missfit. Everyone in the musical town could sing or play. He could do neither. While the others performed, he sat whittling with his knife. One day he met Nicola Amati, a highly respected man in town who had succeeded in the musical field and yet could neither sing or play—he was a violin maker. Amati accepted Stradivari as a pupil and the rest of the story is history.

You may have a "Stradivari" in the rough. Start today to help your child discover his talents by opening to him doors of possibility. Spark that blaze of interest to match his God-given talents and you will help to make it possible for your child to reach his potential.

Step 2: Setting goals.

What if Sir Edmund Hillary on the expedition up Mt. Everest had said, "I doubt if we can make it to the top. Nobody has ever climbed that high"? Someone else's name would have been recorded in the *Guinness Book of*

World Records. What if Beethoven had said, "Whoever heard of a deaf composer? I guess I'll just give up"? Millions would have been denied the great strains of his Ninth Symphony. What if Apostle Paul had said, "Now that I'm in prison I'm too cold and stiff to write any letters"? A good portion of the New Testament would never have been written.

Goals. You've got to have a goal if you're ever going to get anyplace. And if children are ever going to achieve what God has intended, they must set their sites high and reach toward the standard.

How high should children's goals be? Should they aim for intellectual greatness, a Wimbleton championship, a congressional seat, a Nobel prize, or literary fame? Yes, if their motive is to better serve others and to use their God-given talents to glorify their Creator.

God needs great men and women. He has given each one gifts and talents. He doesn't want His gifts wasted. The moral of the story about the talents was that the Lord expected those talents to grow to their greatest capacity. To bury a talent was a sin. I don't want my child to receive the rebuke, "You wicked, lazy servant," for failing to use the skills and abilities with which he or she has been endowed. True greatness doesn't mean necessarily having a name and position. It means developing the talents that God has given each person and putting these to a worthwhile use. Setting a goal is an important step in developing these talents.

A goal gives a focus to life—something on which to concentrate time and energy. Few of the great discoveries and achievements were made by accident. Planning and perseverence were essential. As Edison once said, "Genius is 2% inspiration and 98% perspiration." Without a goal the 98% perspiration just wouldn't be there.

So encourage your child to set goals and develop his talents to the fullest. Inspire him to aim high by reading stories of others who have set goals and achieved what some considered the impossible. The history books are full of accounts of individuals like George Washington Carver, Benjamin Franklin, Thomas Edison, and Madame Curie. Never miss an opportunity to introduce your children to modern-day greats, such as Wilma Rudolph who was told as a child she would never walk. But her goal was to run. And she did—carrying away an Olympic gold metal in track. And then there is Joni Eareckson, a quadraplegic who determined to draw holding a pen in her teeth. Her drawings are now a testimony to millions about what God has done in her life. In each one of these individuals a God-given talent was present, but would have lain dormant without the individual setting a goal and putting in the "perspiration" necessary to make it come true.

Your child may not be a Benjamin Franklin or a Madame Curie, but he or she can achieve what others cannot, because God has destined each to a special work and endowed each with talents necessary for success. Encourage your child to aim high so he can be a blessing to others and a worthy servant of his Master. Goal setting will make the development of his God-given talents possible.

Step 3: Reaching for the stars—achieving goals.

Stars have a way of guiding people where they want to go. Astronauts plot their positions by punching data from the stars into their computers. Columbus sailed to America using the North star for calculations. And years before, the Star of Bethlehem led the wisemen to the Babe in the manger.

Goals are like stars. They're easy to look at, tempting to wish for, hard to reach, but essential for getting where you want to go. It is one thing to inspire a child to set goals in life—but quite another to encourage a child to reach them. The journey toward achieving a goal is like reaching for a star. Here are some guidelines for your children.

1. Reach for the closest star first. Help your child to set reasonable short-term goals. A long-term goal is fine—but it may be so far away that discouragement will set in before the goal is realized. Children thrive on accomplishments that short-term goals make possible. Help your child make a list of what he would like to accomplish each day. When a goal is reached, cross it off—celebrate. Break larger goals into little pieces. Then each small accomplishment can be seen as one step nearer to success.

2. Reach for only one star at a time. It's easy for a child to get trapped into trying to accomplish too many goals at once. Ten projects are started and one completed. Starting and never finishing is a bad habit to fall into. So remember this motto:

> One thing at a time and that done well
> Is a very good thing as all may tell.
> Work with your will and all your might.
> Things done by halves are never done right.

3. Encourage your child to reach toward the star of his choice. To have the motivation necessary for success, the goal must be the child's, not yours. At times you may be reluctant to encourage because the child's goal is different from what you had in mind. You thought he'd become a missionary; instead he majored in art. You hoped he'd be musical, but collecting butterflies is where his interest lies. You planned she would study medicine, but she loves construction. Encourage your child to set goals based on his natural talents and interests.

4. Celebrate when a star has been reached. Show appre-

ciation for goals achieved. Compliment the child. Pat him on the back. Call a family celebration. Take a picture to record the event. Give her a "hip-hip-hurrah." Help the child feel intrinsically good about his accomplishment by saying, "It makes you feel good when you've reached your goal, doesn't it?" Then praise God for making it all possible.

5. Finally, there may be some goals that your child will set that will be impossible to reach. Rather than feeling a failure, help him realize that it was better to have set the goal and tried, than to have never had the goal at all. Look at the benefits by having reached toward the goal, even though at this time the goal may lie beyond. Doing your best is what counts. Remember, goals are like stars. You may never reach them, but you can set your course by them. It is the reaching toward the stars that makes the achieving of goals possible.

Paul said, "I can do all things through Christ which strengtheneth me." (Philippians 4:13.) And the promise is, ". . . with God all things are possible." (Mark 10:27.) Let's help our children develop their God-given potential. If we do our best, God can do the rest.

The Importance of Parental Encouragement

Close your eyes and pretend your grown son is out flying a kite in an electrical storm. What would you say if you were Ben Franklin's mother? "Can you imagine a man his age out flying a kite in a thunderstorm. He's crazy; that's what he is. You'd think he would spend his time doing something worthwhile. He's going to get himself killed with all that lightning!" Not many mothers would say, "Keep it up, Ben. You'll be successful yet. There must be some way to harness all that electricity."

How would your child rate you on a scale from highly encouraging to highly discouraging? It is easy to discourage a child. We do it by being overly critical, by expecting perfection, by being pessimistic, by expressing unrealistic fears, by nagging and by pointing out weaknesses rather than strengths.

A child's feelings about himself are a reflection of how he perceives others feel about him. Your confidence and encouragement will tell him you see his potential. Sometimes children de-value themselves. Counter their negatives by pointing out their positives. Don't allow self-depreciation to defeat your child's chances of success. Make sure your child feels like the ten-talent person he is.

It's not always easy for a child to develop his talents. It takes practice and perseverance. And sometimes the only thing that keeps children moving ahead when the going gets tough is knowing their parents have confidence in them.

Barnabas was an encourager. He took John-Mark under his wings when Paul, fed up with his immaturity, wouldn't give him a second chance. Barnabas saw his potential. Barnabas saw what he could become with the right training and leadership. (Acts 15:37-39.) And with Barnabas' encouragement John-Mark fulfilled his expectations and became a valuable worker for God—and a help to Paul! (2 Timothy 4:11.)

Jesus was an encourager. He gave the hopeless hope. Look how He treated Mary Magdalene. Others considered her worthless. Jesus saw infinite possibilities in her. And Mary was so overwhelmed that she spent her entire life savings to show her gratitude. (John 8:3-11.)

My dad, too, was an encourager. His confidence in me challenged me to accomplishments few other children my age had a chance to even try. When I was in junior high I began working at my father's manufacturing plant after school. I was just a kid. Dad paid me out of his pocket, since I was too young to draw a salary. But Dad never felt I was too young to learn what I wanted to learn. He allowed me to sit next to the most experienced assembly line workers, he taught me to use the punch presses and other heavy machinery, and later he allowed me to graduate to the billing and purchasing department. At times I was scared I would make a costly error. But Dad believed that mistakes were the stuff out of which character is built. Either you use a mistake as an excuse to give up or as a stepping stone to success. And when I did make a mistake, I never remember him being angry. "Try again," he encouraged. "You can do anything you set your mind to, Kay, if you work hard enough."

Encourage, encourage, encourage. Inspire your child with confidence. Nothing is so deflating as a parent who stands by lamenting, "I knew you couldn't do it." Your child can be a ten-talent kid. With your encouragement he can reach his potential.

Encourage intellectual curiosity. One of the most sought after talents in the scientific world is intellectual curiosity. Someone who isn't satisfied with the known, but is searching for new answers and creative solutions.

Children are born curious—always reaching for that which is beyond, taking objects apart to see what makes them tick, and asking a thousand times a day, "Why? Why? Why?" If children are born this way, why do we have so few intellectually curious adults?

Burton White, a foremost authority on young children, says there are two things at risk in children during the first three years. The first is language development and the second, curiosity. Very early we have a way of inhibiting or diminishing this important talent in children.

One way we discourage curiosity is to punish a child for exploring. We spank him for getting dirty, rather than listening to his exciting story about digging in the mud and finding night-crawlers. We chastise her for exposing the film rather than accepting the experience as an inexpensive lesson on the operation of a camera.

Another good way to discourage the explorer is to make it unsafe. If the backyard isn't fenced and you're afraid of the neighbor's dog and Daddy doesn't have time to supervise, it's safer to stay inside.

Even our choice of inside toys discourages experimentation and creativity. How much imagination does a doll stimulate if it can do everything by itself? And these fancy toys break so easily, smart children leave them on the shelf rather than take the chance of a broken toy arrousing Mom's wrath.

It takes time to think and to explore. When we plan our children's days so tightly with lessons of every shape and description, we don't leave much time for creative play and for satisfying intellectual curiosity. Instead we give children all the right answers. We flood them with information—even before they are interested. We teach them the exciting fact that an A is an A and other abstractions that have little meaning.

If we really cared about our children developing intellectual curiosity, we would quit telling them so much and start encouraging them to discover answers for themselves.

Jean Piaget was a famous developmental psychologist who has written more about cognitive development than any other man in history. One day his daughter was twirling around and became dizzy. "Daddy," she asked looking up at him, "are things going around for you as they are for me?" Most of us would consider this the teachable moment to explain the intricacies of the balance mechanism and the workings of the inner ear. But not Piaget. Instead he asked, "What do you think?" She shrugged her shoulders and replied, "I don't know." But that wasn't the end. The next day she ran up to her daddy shouting, "I think I know the answer. Things aren't moving around for you because I'm not tall enough to stir up that much air."

What is more important, the right answer or the thought process? If Piaget would have explained the facts immediately he would have cut off the thinking involved in discovering a solution. Facts are important—but their importance lie in one's ability to use them. Facts are most meaningful when we use them to discover new knowledge and creative solutions.

Encourage curiosity. Make it safe to explore. Provide sturdy, stimulating toys that inspire creativity, imagination and discovery. Allow time for your child to explore. And then instead of providing all the answers, ask a few more questions and encourage youngsters to discover the solu-ions. Within every child God implanted intellectual curiosity. Let's do everything possible to insure a rich and fruitful harvest.

Helping Children Learn Right From Wrong

Teaching right from wrong—it's relatively easy when a child is a baby and parental commandments are law. Just consistently say "no." Reinforce your words with action and if you persist for a long enough time, the do's and don'ts finally sink in.

God knew how this could be accomplished best. He said, "And these words, which I command thee this day, shall be in thine heart: And thou shalt teach them diligently unto thy children, and shalt talk of them when thou sittest in thine house, and when thou walkest by the way, and when thou liest down, and when thou risest up. And thou shalt bind them for a sign upon thine hand, and they shall be as frontlets between thine eyes. And thou shalt write them upon the posts of thy house, and on thy gate." (Deuteronomy 6:6-9.) There was no way His children could forget the commandments if this instruction were followed.

The problem comes after you have done all of the above; the children know the right answers and yet like Paul, they do what they don't want to do and don't do what they should! (Romans 7:15.) When this happens it's time to introduce them to the sin problem and the tremendous influence Satan has upon our lives, tempting us at our weakest point; how he's walking around like a roaring lion seeking whom he may devour. (1 Peter 5:8.)

I've seen children try hard to be good. At bedtime they ask for forgiveness and promise to be good; they announce at breakfast that they're not going to do anything wrong all day. But before the dishes are washed, they have already pulled brother's hair, angrily emptied the trash in the middle of the floor, and blamed the trash pile on sister who was playing outside. Hostile expressions of anger, revenge and lying, minutes after the declaration of lifetime affection, obedience, good-will and honesty.

When this happens it's time to read to your children Susan Davis's book *Naughty Heart, Clean Heart* (Review and Herald Publishing Association, 1978). It's about little ones who try so hard to be good. They promise and fail. On their own they can never be good. Satan is just too clever and strong. By themselves they don't have a chance to win against the enemy. But Jesus has already won the battle. And if they ask Jesus to come into their lives and fight their battles for them—they can have success.

In a simple way the book teaches children the importance of righteousness by faith. "Ask and it shall be given unto you, seek and you shall find, knock and it shall be opened unto you." (Matthew 7:7.) Instead of working so hard to be good by ourselves, we must accept Christ's help and His promise to change our lives. He will take our filthy-rag righteousness away and place His perfect robe of righteousness around us. (Isaiah 61:10.)

Children must learn to stop trying to be good by themselves and **begin asking God for power to overcome the tempter.** Encourage children to form a partnership with Jesus. It's a winning combination.

When there is a clear right and wrong to an issue, it's fairly easy to expect obedience. But what about shades of grey?

A child's ability to discern right from wrong develops with age. At first the child only sees the black and white of an issue. He follows the letter of the law. Later the child begins to understand the importance of the principles behind the rules and the motives for a person's behavior.

It was a scorching hot day in Southern California. We had gone for a walk through the hot, dusty fields and returned sweaty and covered with dirt. It was Sabbath afternoon and time for my preschoolers to nap. I didn't like the idea of having them tracking dust through the house and messing up the sink in order to scrub away the dirt. That would mean work for me and I wanted to obey the Biblical command to not work on the Sabbath. (Exodus 20:8-11.) So I suggested that the children dip into the swimming pool and wash off before their naps.

They looked at me as if I had lost my mind. "Mother," they exclaimed, "you're not going to let us go swimming on Sabbath, are you?" To them, "No swimming on Sabbath," was an unbreakable rule. They were not yet old enough to discern that behind the rule was the principle that we should make Sabbath special and refrain from our own frivilous play and only participate in activities that brought us closer to God. But to the children, getting into the swimming pool water was wrong!

Because young children have a difficult time understanding principles and motives, it's better for parents to live a consistent life. Otherwise, the children tend to be confused by all the exceptions to the rules. But at the same time be quick to explain the reasons behind the rules, rather than expecting blind obedience. Talk about a person's motives. Many times people do wrong because they don't know any better. Or they want to help, yet in their awkward way end up hurting someone. People make mistakes. The accidental wrong is very different from the person who deliberately sets out to seek revenge or defy the rules.

One more area is confusing to children. They tend to equate the severity of the punishment received to the wrongness of the act. For example, ask a child, "Which boy was the worst boy . . . Johnny, who found a wallet and asked his Daddy to find the owner and his Daddy gave him a spanking, or Billy who found a wallet and used the money to buy himself an ice cream cone?" The spanking is confusing and more than likely the child will say Johnny was the worst because of the punishment he received. Let's help children learn right from wrong by making our discipline just. If the wrong was accidental, let's be understanding. If it's deliberate, there should be a logical consequence.

As children approach the teen years they must begin thinking through issues for themselves, making their own decision about whether something is right or wrong. If parents remain dictatorial, unreasonably requiring obedience to rules that children feel are unjust and archaic, children are likely to rebel.

Teenagers' reasoning can be shrewd. Their questions are sometimes difficult to answer without interjecting personal values. Simplistic answers are no longer satisfying. They begin to see the inconsistencies in adult lives and label parents "hypocrites" in order to find an excuse for their own wayward behavior.

The only way to avoid confrontation is to be willing to openly discuss issues. Have a clear rationale behind your values. Avoid arguments. If you are consistent and base your decisions on principles, your children will respect you, even though they may not agree with your value system. You might even be pleasantly surprised to overhear them using your arguments in a discussion with a friend.

Finally, how do you handle the really hard questions, like what's wrong with disco dancing or X-rated movies? Often after parents present all the reasons they can think of, children are still not convinced. They argue that dancing is good exercise and questionable movies have been viewed at home, why not the theater? Or they say, "Mom, you've never been there. How can you know?"

Rather than be caught in a "pharisaical trap" or an endless argument, why not try Jesus' way; tell them the parable of the Skylark.

> Once upon a time there was a Skylark family who spent a good share of the day searching for food. One day Jr. Skylark heard a little man calling, "Two worms for a Skylark feather." "Wow," thought Jr. Skylark, "That sounds like a good deal. I have plenty of feathers." So he hopped over to the little man, plucked out a feather and received two juicy worms.
>
> Jr. Skylark didn't like working for his dinner, so every day he hopped over to the little man and traded his feathers for worms.
>
> Soon summer passed and the nights began to grow cold. It was almost time to fly south. Jr. Skylark, with so few feathers, felt the chill more than the rest. He was eager to leave. Finally, moving day came. Mom and Dad Skylark flew into the air calling for their children to follow. Everyone took off except Jr. He struggled and struggled to get airborne. But alas, he didn't have enough feathers to fly. He had traded his feathers for worms.

What is wrong with disco dancing and X-rated movies? Nothing, if you plan on just living a life on earth. But if you plan on heaven, then disco dancing and X-rated movies don't enhance one's relationship with the person who has made heaven possible. It doesn't bring you closer to Christ. *It all depends on your destination.*

Talk about your teenager's destination. Encourage them to plan ways they can move in the direction they want to go and be ready for the trip rather than trading their feathers for the worms of this world.

Knowing and Needing God

Knowing the rules and strategies of soccer will never make you a professional athlete. Memorizing the keyboard is not a guarantee that you'll be a 100 word per minute typist. And knowing how to mix and apply paint to a canvas won't make you an artist. Knowing (cognitive understanding) alone is a fairly low level of learning.

What really counts is what you do with your knowledge. And so it is with a child's spirituality. Knowing the right answers or being awed by someone elses story of conversion will never assure your child's salvation. It's personal practice that counts. Acting on what you know—experiencing the Christian life yourself—is what is really important. Spiritual growth comes by doing something with your knowledge.

Parents, help your child personally experience God working in their lives. Don't wait for the big miracles before acknowledging God. Note the times God helps them get their room cleaned before company comes, or helps them find the lost turtle, or helps them speak calmly when they felt like screaming.

Be open to share what God is doing for you. Start a

family prayer list and let the family rejoice with each answer. Keep a spiritual diary, recording how God is working in your home. Read it over at the end of each week and thank the Lord for His involvement in the lives of each family member.

Talk to God to keep you company instead of turning on the TV or radio. Let your child hear you pray—not cliches, but specific, meaningful conversational prayers.

Praise God even when things aren't going your way. "God, thanks for this parking place, even though it's three blocks from where I need to be. You must have known I needed some exercise."

Don't always be the one who plans and conducts worship. Give the assignment away for others to take the responsibility. Daily Bible study often occurs only at family worship time. Encourage private devotions, even for your preschoolers. If you always take the responsibility to make sure the children study their Bible lessons seven times a week, the system may break down when you're not around. Personal responsibility is essential. Encourage your children to call you to study, instead of you always having to remind them.

A child will never make it through to the kingdom on second-hand religion. Knowing isn't enough. Only personal experience will assure a growing, vital and lasting relationship with their heavenly Father.

Needing God

Establishing a personal relationship with God will encourage the child to trust and depend on Him. When a child contrasts his goodness to God's goodness, the need for God becomes more apparent.

We all need God. But we don't often realize it until we feel helpless; when we can't solve our own problems; when we're not smart enough, strong enough, or skillful enough to get ourselves out of trouble. Naaman didn't think he needed God until he got leprosy. In desperation he turned to God—and God came through. God saved him. (See 2 Kings 5.) We can do a lot of things for ourselves—but we can't save ourselves. Our greatest need is for God's salvation.

Built into every child is the desire, "I want to do it myself." This feeling helps a child grow toward the independence and self-sufficiency needed to become a healthy adult. But it gets in a child's way when he becomes so self-sufficient that he no longer feels he needs God.

Must every child have a "leprosy-crisis" to realize he is not completely self-sufficient—that he can't save himself from his sins and give himself eternal life? This isn't necessary. Nor do parents have to wait until the child can understand abstract concepts before presenting the plan of salvation. The concept of God's salvation is so simple that children of every age can understand their need for salvation and accept Christ as the fulfillment of this need. In fact, it is easier for a child to accept these truths if taught early than if kept until the teenager is secure in his own self-sufficiency.

Let's make God real to our children. And start early. The preschooler is a ready audience. Young children realize they need "somebody bigger" to take care of them. They can grasp fantasy as easily as reality. They don't have to see to believe. Their faith is bigger than this. Santa Claus, the Good Fairy, and Mother Nature are real people to the innocent preschooler—often more real than God. Why? Television and storybooks picture these fantasy characters. Everyone talks about them. When we take advantage of a child's unquestioning trust and present fantasy as truth, what must he think of us when we later begin telling him about a God he's never seen?

Why not make God, who really does exist, a living vital person to a child from birth. Make God so real that children begin talking to God as they do their imaginary friends. But unless God is real to you, you'll probably spend more time reading to your children about Superman and Darth Vader! Check yourself. How real is God to you? Do your children hear you talking to God throughout the day as to a friend? Do they hear you telling about what God is doing for you? Have they heard you accept Christ's gift of salvation—and have they seen this make a difference in the way you live?

Salvation. Justification. Sanctification. The words may boggle your mind. Search for understanding yourself. Then make these abstract concepts simple and concrete for your child—just as Christ did—by telling stories. Read to your child about Cain, Abel and Abraham. These stories point to the need of Christ's sacrifice for us. Death may sound cruel but it is a consequence of sin. Look around you. Nature can dramatize this reality. Then explain God's answer for death—the gift of salvation—with an object lesson. Hold out a $5 bill. Say, "It is yours if you accept it." The child will probably ask, "What strings are attached?" "None," you will answer. "The money is yours if you will accept it." "Why?" your child will question. "Because I love you." That is exactly how the gift of salvation is given to us. It is free, no strings attached. Christ has already died for us. All we have to do is accept His gift and we will never have to die that eternal death. That is how much God loves us!

A child's greatest spiritual need is to be saved. God is saying to each one of His children, "Look unto me, and be ye saved, all the ends of the earth: for I am God, and there is none else." (Isaiah 45:22.) Let's make sure that God's invitation is delivered to each of His children! We want all of God's kids to be able to spend eternity together with Him.

Teaching Children to Talk to God

"Pray without ceasing." (1 Thessalonians 5:17.) A great memory verse for every child of God.

Too often praying is a ritual children perform at bedtime and before meals and once a week at church. What our children really need is to learn how to talk with God all day long, not just when they are expected to say, "I'm sorry," "Please give me," or "Thank You."

I doubt if you'd have many friends if you only talked to them when you'd done something wrong, when you needed something, or when you wanted to say thank you. Relationships grow on chit-chat, brainstorming, discussing ideas and plans, telling stories and jokes, sharing feelings, laughing and crying together.

Why not talk with God this same way? Help your children express their true feelings and put a little life into their prayers. I'll guarantee that their relationship with God will grow. Here's how to begin:

1. *Teach your child to be a creative conversationalist.*

"Have you said your prayers yet?" one Mom asked her seven-year-old as she bent over to kiss him goodnight.

"Well, not exactly," he replied. "I decided God must

get pretty tired listening to the same old thing, so tonight I told Him the story of Goldilocks and the Three Bears."

Why not? I think my God would be pleased we cared enough to share something with Him we thought He'd really enjoy.

Memorized prayers don't really turn me on—I wonder what God thinks when we bow our heads and out tumble the same old words. You don't even have to think about what you are saying. It's like a child saying mealtime grace and repeating the words, "Now I lay me down to sleep . . ." or blessing the food at bedtime.

Putting your mind in neutral to recite cliches is meaningless. One little girl prayed, "God bless Bingo, Trixie, and Uncle Eddie has a farm E-I-E-I-O." What must God think when He hears us mumble our rote-learned prayers while our mind is on a baseball game or Susie's fancy dress?

One night after my nine-year-old had prayed the same prayer I had heard every night for the last seven years, I asked, "Kevin, do you think God has ever heard that prayer before?"

"Yes," he admitted. "I prayed the same thing last night."

"Is that the only other time?"

"No," he smiled. "I prayed it the night before that, and the night before that, too."

"Kevin, do you tell your best friends the very same thing every day?"

"No, Mom. I tell them important things—like who won the soccer game and how to tie a square knot and why batteries go dead."

"Kevin, God is your very best friend. Don't you think He might like to hear something new—something that's really important—like the things you tell your best friends?''

''I don't know,'' said Keven, shrugging his shoulders, ''I never thought about that.''

''God is interested in everything that happens to you,'' I continued, ''and He wants to answer your prayers. You might not be able to hear Him, but you can think an answer and then continue talking. Just to give you an idea what really talking to God is like, pray again and I'll answer what I think God might answer.''

Kevin began again, ''Dear God, I had a great time with Tim today.''

I answered, ''God might say to you, 'Kevin, I'm happy you did. Tell me, what did you do together?' ''

''Oh, we started building a tree house.''

''That sounds like fun—and hard work.''

''Yea, it was hard work, but it's safe. We braced the boards and jumped on them to make sure they wouldn't come loose.''

''That was a good idea. What else did you do?''

Kevin continued his prayer. After about five minutes—which seemed like an eternity to me—I interjected, ''Kevin, Mommy has worked hard all day and I still have the dishes to do. Do you think we could say goodnight for now so I can get back to my work?''

''Sure,'' replied Kevin. ''Talking to God is a lot more fun this way.''

The next morning my husband asked Kevin to say grace. ''Dear God,'' he began, ''Thank You for the good night's sleep—and for the terrific dream. I dreamed that we had a giant water slide in our backyard—and a wave pool—a huge one just for me. It was just like the ocean. And I'm glad we get to go on a field trip today. I hope I don't have to sit next to a girl on the bus. Don't let me forget to ask

Dad for a dollar to buy something special. I hope they still have the mynah bird at the entrance to the zoo. Maybe he'll whistle at me. And . . ."

By this time the girls were fidgeting. If they didn't get the food blessed soon they would be late for school. "Kevin, the food—bless the food," Kim whispered.

Obviously, Kevin was enjoying his new relationship with God; and the girls did get to school on time. The few extra minutes it took to tell God about his dream and the field trip were well worth it. It perked up our usual morning routine—and I'm sure it made God smile.

2. *Teach your child to talk with God about what is currently on his mind and heart.*

God wants to hear about the headliners in our lives today. And He wants to add His commentary, if we'll just talk with Him and not at Him.

How do you feel right now? Bubbly all over, crabby, impish, discouraged, silly, ready to tackle the world, like your best friend has deserted you? Tell God about it. He's interested. To help children tune into their feelings have sharing times during the day. Ask the question, "How are you feeling right now?" and then together kneel right down and tell God about those feelings. Before jumping up, wait a minute, be quiet with God and listen for His reaction. Ask your child, "What did God say?" and expect an answer.

Our girls Kim and Kari were wrestling and giggling instead of going to sleep as their dad had asked them to do. When I could stand it no longer I marched into their room like a general and commanded, "Stop immediately or you're going to get it!" Quiet reigned.

Then I asked in a different tone of voice, "Have you girls said your prayers?" They knelt down and Kari prayed earnestly, "Dear Jesus, please help Mommy not to be so strict!" She said what was on her mind and I helped God answer that prayer by apologizing for my behavior and tucking them gently into bed with a good night kiss.

3. *Teach your child to pray for others.*

When Kevin was four he noticed a woman in a neck brace and prayed, "Dear Jesus, please help the lady with the neck cast to get it off." I thought the prayer was cute and mentioned it to the woman. A couple weeks later Kevin received a letter, "Dear Kevin. Since you prayed for me I haven't had to wear my neck brace. Thank you."

"God answered my prayer!" Kevin shouted as he danced around the room.

It is special when God answers our prayers for ourselves and we get a new bicycle or party dress, but nothing can match the joy the child experiences when God answers his or her prayers for someone else. Help your child make a prayer list. Encourage him to pray systematically for others; teach her to claim Bible promises for those in need. Remind your youngster to thank God for answered prayer.

It won't take your child long to find a new friend in God when he begins creatively talking with Him, sharing what's really current in his thoughts or feelings and telling God about his other friends and loved ones.

Why not encourage your child to have a little talk with God right now?

Worship — Celebration or Frustration?

"Oh come, let us worship and bow down: let us kneel before the Lord our maker. For he is our God; and we are the people of his pasture, and the sheep of his hand." Psalm 95:6, 7.

Worship should be the most joyous occasion of the week. "Serve the Lord with gladness: come before his presence with singing." Psalm 100:2. Is this how your children view the worship experience?

The next time you attend your church worship service, look around you. What are the children learning? Are they learning to worship—to show God how much they love Him? Or are they learning that the worship service is a time to catch up on their reading, to hear the latest gossip, or get a little sleep? If they modeled the adults' behavior, would they be dynamic worshipers or would they merely be existing until the benediction released them from the burdensome ritual? What are their parents teaching them? To praise God meaningfully or to sit still or they'll get it after church? What attitudes are they forming about worship? That it's boring and meaningless or that it's a relevant part of a love relationship with one's Creator?

Worship should be a spontaneous expression of love to God. The result should be a closer, more personal relationship. After all, to worship is to come into the very presence of God. Being filled with God's Spirit should make us bubble over with so much love that we cannot contain it. Our after-worship thoughts should be to share this love with others.

Let's face it. There are numerous lukewarm Christians filling church pews. Do not let your child be confused into thinking that what he sees these persons doing at church is truly worship. Set your own standards. Encourage active participation. Prepare your child for the worship experience. After meeting with God for worship, plan a follow-up experience so worship can go beyond the four walls of the sanctuary. Make the church worship service a celebration of love. Make it so meaningful your child won't want to miss it.

Set your own standards for worship behavior. When children are small they will behave in ways appropriate for their age. For example, a 12-month-old will cry when hungry or tired. A 20-month-old doesn't know what the word *quiet* means and may practice his new vocabulary at inappropriate times. Most 3-year-olds I know are fidgeters. Sitting still is just not a part of their repertoire.

When children cannot meet your standards for reverence, step out with them so other worshipers are not disturbed. But use your time-out period to worship with the child—in a way he can better understand. Smell flowers, follow the path of the ants, or pick up pretty pebbles—and talk about the Creator. Have prayer right there and thank Jesus. Encourage the child to want to return to God's house by having a special book or activity that is only for church.

Make church attractive. Make it meaningful—not a

place where threats of punishment hang over a child's head if he makes a wrong move. God doesn't want unhappy, resistant worshipers, but cheerful, enthusiastic ones.

Encourage Participation

As children grow, encourage participation. Call the church secretary to find out the hymns and the Scripture text to be used in the worship service. Learn the songs. Have the child mark the text in his Bible so he is ready to find it when it's read in church. Explain its meaning beforehand. Have him earn his offering by doing jobs around the house. Pay him in pennies so he can figure out his tithe easily. Help him fill out the offering envelope so he is ready to participate in this part of the service.

Older children should be encouraged to take notes on the sermon. I suggest following the sermon with a pencil and an open Bible. Underline texts used. Write marginal notes explaining the text.

If children are not ready to follow the sermon word for word, discourage the reading of church papers or the drawing of unrelated pictures. Instead, encourage Bible study. It is an act of worship. Write down questions and have the children find the answers in the Bible. If they draw, they can draw pictures to illustrate the sermon, and then you can use these as you talk about the sermon later in the day. Set your own standards of church behavior. If you don't you'll notice your children modeling after the poor examples of others. Few follow the good.

Take time to prepare your children for church before each worship experience. Avoid the last-minute rush to make it to the church on time. Critical words and angry admonitions don't prepare the heart for worship.

Get ready early and plan a family prechurch activity such as walking or bicycling instead of driving to church, if practical. Make it a nature trip or notice pretty homes and gardens and choose those things that you think you would like someday in your heavenly home.

Our family enjoys inviting guests for Sabbath breakfast. Good fellowship and food and a planned morning-worship experience at home make God's day start in a special way. At other times we enjoy a picnic breakfast in the country on our way to church.

Immediately before the sanctuary worship service, take time again to prepare your child for worship. If he needs exercise, take a short walk. Read him a story if you know his habit is to nag for one during the service. Have a special family prayer for God's Spirit to come to each person in a special way during the service. With such preparation, children are looking for a blessing and meaning in the service, and the chances are much greater that they will find it.

After church, talk about the worship service. How was your prayer answered about being filled with God's Spirit? What did you get out of the sermon? What thought do you want to remember all week? What "marching orders" did you receive?

Then plan how your family can apply the words of the sermon and make it practical. What changes do you need to make in your lives? What special activity can you do today? For example, if the sermon was on thoughtfulness, what thoughtful thing can your family do for someone that very afternoon?

If you feel your worship service has been planned for adults only, suggest these ideas to the pastor or elder to encourage participation of the younger set:

1. Include a short children's sermon, story, or object lesson.

2. Start a thanksgiving service in which children can testify about what God has done for them. This may be at thank-offering time.

3. Choose junior greeters or deacons to help adults usher and take up the offering. You don't have to be 40 to do these tasks.

4. Start a children's choir or include a musical selection given by children.

5. Ask the pastor to develop questions about the sermon that the children can answer while listening. This may help a few adults to pay attention, too.

6. Prepare a children's bulletin that can be filled in weekly. Sample questions might include: What was the title of the opening hymn? Where was the Scripture text found? What were three important ideas to remember from the sermon? What did you enjoy most about the worship service? Write down the name of one new friend you met.

7. Have families give certain parts of the worship service, such as reading the scripture or giving special music.

8. Occasionally let the youth plan and present a service.

10. Let the children circulate through the congregation, gathering a special offering for a children's program or educational activity.

11. Once each month have a family worship in which the whole program is geared to the family—something for the young as well as the old.

12. Encourage the pastor to have children participate in the sermon by asking them questions or involving them in an object lesson.

13. Consider starting a children's church program for part or all of the worship service. This may be an ideal

training time for teaching reverence and encouraging participation.

By careful preparation and planning, you can make the church worship service meaningful for your children. Let's make it a celebration of love.

Making Heaven a Great Place To Go

John the Revelator saw heaven. I can only imagine its splendor. Here is what he described: "And I John saw the holy city, new Jerusalem coming down from God out of heaven, prepared as a bride adorned for her husband . . . and the building of the wall of it was of jasper: and the city was pure gold, like unto clear glass. And the foundations of the wall of the city were garnished with all manner of precious stones . . . And the city had no need of the sun, neither of the moon, to shine in it: for the glory of God did lighten it. . . . And he showed me a pure river of water of life, clear as crystal, proceeding out of the throne of God and of the Lamb . . . and on either side of the river, was there the tree of life, which bare twelve manner of fruits, and yielded her fruit every month . . ." (Selected verses from Revelation 21, 22.)

What a place! What a reward for those who keep His commandments and accept His gift of salvation.

Christian parents are anxious for heaven—but what about God's kids?

Have you ever had a hard time convincing your child that he should want to go to heaven? The stereotype picture of heaven with children dressed in spotless white robes in the middle of a manicured garden does not look very appealing to kids that love wearing jeans and making mud pies or throwing snowballs.

Let's make heaven attractive to children. Let's do away with these misconceptions.

Misconception #1: In heaven you live alone in a mansion. Young children have said, "I don't want to go to heaven. I'm scared to be alone. I like my own house. I don't want to live in a mansion." A child's security is built around his family and his home. The familiar. Preschoolers ask, "Mommy, can I still live with you when I get big and you're my Grandma?" It's disconcerting to think of moving away from your own house, your own bed, pillow and teddy bear. It is frightening to think about going someplace alone.

For a preschooler, heaven should be a home for the whole family, where Daddy can play with you all day and where there will be no spankings. For teens, who are pushing for freedom, heaven can be a place where they can have their own mansion, with a swimming pool and tennis court, and they can invite over whomever they want—24 hours a day.

Misconception #2: God only resurrects people—not pets. When a child looses a pet, the finality of death can be devastating. A pet can become a child's closest confidant —a part of his life he will never forget. Where did we get the idea that pets aren't going to heaven? My God is such a big God that if He knows heaven won't be heaven without Rover or Fluffy, don't worry, they'll be there. My God can do anything!

Misconception #3: You can't have any fun in heaven doing what you enjoy most. "Why should I want to go to heaven? There's nothin' to do there except float around on clouds, pet lions and play golden harps. And I hate to practice!''

One day Grandpa bought Kevin a slingshot. At bedtime Kevin was still having so much fun he wanted to carry it to bed. After prayers, Kevin asked, ''Grandma, will Jesus have a slingshot for me in heaven?''

''I don't know for sure, Kevin. But if Jesus knows how much you want one, He'll probably have one there for you.''

Kevin thought for a moment and replied, ''I think I'll take mine along just to make sure. Then if Jesus has one for me, I'll lay mine down.''

Why can't God have motorcycles, wave pools and cross country skiing available? My children once heard a minister say he wanted to float down the River of Life on an inner tube. What fun! Three Kuzma kids now want to tag along. Make that five Kuzmas—I think Jan and I would like that, too!

Let's talk about heaven. Let's brainstorm about what we're going to do there. The sky isn't the limit in heaven. Let's make heaven so appealing that this old world looks drab and dull in comparison. Let's set our sights on heaven and all determine to meet there someday on the right side of the throne of God.

The Family Heritage

The Scriptures say, "In the beginning, God . . ." (Genesis 1:1.) But God did not want to be alone and so He said, "Let us make man in our image, after our likeness . . ." (Genesis 1:26.) God's kids have a wonderful heritage!

In the fast changing world of today children need a sense of who they are, where they've come from, and where they're going.

Share with them their spiritual family heritage. God is their Father, Jesus their Brother. And then introduce them to the long line of Bible famous relatives right back to Adam and Eve.

Young children are God's children. What an honor! How valuable they should feel to know that God created them and gives them each a body-guard angel. (Only important people have body-guards!) And then because God knew they would break His law and have to die, He planned ahead and sent Jesus, their Brother, to die for them. He has a plan to save them so they can live with God in heaven if they'll only accept His gift of salvation.

What a privilege to be the son or daughter of God! What a lot to live up to. What a heritage and what a future to look forward to—eternity living as a part of God's family.

Now, be more specific and share your own personal family heritage. Introduce your children to their past. Tell stories of grandparents, great-grandparents and as far back as you can recall. Point out their ancestor's admirable traits and the lessons they can learn from the not so admirable traits.

Create a family identity by making a family tree, pasting on pictures of relatives and explaining their relationships. Then plan a family reunion or a trip across the country so the people on the "tree" can become real people for your children.

Do you have a family crest, coat of arms, logo, or symbol? If not, design one. Use this on a banner, a hook-latch rug, a wooden plaque or your own stationery. Why not have your own family stationery printed. I received a letter recently on letter-head stationery. "From the home office of the McDowell Company: President (father's name), Executive vice-president (mother's name), Junior partners (children's names). What a great idea!

Write your immediate family's history. Start with your marriage. Have a chapter on the birth or adoption of each child. Then annually write a new chapter. As the children get older, have them write certain sections, such as, "What my mommy and daddy did for me this year," or "Why I'm glad I'm a part of this family."

Talk about what makes your family different from other families. What are your strong character traits, abilities and skills? What special talents has God given your family? How do the individual strengths of each family member contribute to the whole?

Finally discuss where you are going as a family—your plans, your goals. What directions has God given your family from the Bible? What unique contribution do you feel God is calling on your family to make to help others of

His family who don't know Him as well?

As important as the past may be to give children a sense of family heritage—a rudder on a restless sea—it is not as important as the present. Ask your children, "What would you like to be remembered for by **your** children and grandchildren some day?" Help your children to realize that their choices today will determine what they will be tomorrow. God can help them reach their ideals, no matter what their family heritage has been. Encourage them to capitalize on family strengths and ask God, their Father, to help fill the deficiencies so their own children's heritage can be even brighter than theirs. Emphasize the fact that their own future will be determined by their actions today. They, in a sense, are the most important part of their heritage.

Family Dedication

God has a special purpose for every family. By uniting together to achieve a common goal, families can accomplish far more than if each member works alone. But there are so many forces pulling and pushing for attention that the family sometimes gets lost in the shuffle. You want to play together. You want coöperation and loyalty. You want to be working toward the same goal—but what goal is challenging enough to inspire family unity?

What about service to others and God? Could this be a goal that would unite your family?

Let me share an idea. A couple who had each lost a spouse, had recently married, bringing six children together under one roof. How do you begin blending eight people with such varied backgrounds into one family? They decided to dedicate their home to the service of God. They called their pastor and arranged for him to hold a short ceremony. They invited guests. And then to certify the occasion they made a plaque for the family room.

I was impressed. Just having the home dedication plaque on the wall would be a constant reminder to solve problems in a positive way. It would be hard to yell and shout at each other with a dedication plaque so visible. Plus, what a witness to guests about the family's primary goal—service to God.

Why not begin today planning your family's home dedication?

I would like to encourage you to dedicate your family to God by sending you this beautiful 8 x 10 Home Dedication Certificate. (See offer on page 142.) This certificate can be a witness to others of your family's dedication to God and a constant reminder to your family of the purpose to which they were born. And to you, parents, it can help you never to forget the privilege and responsibility you have when living with God's kids.

This Certifies that
the Home of

has been dedicated to God
this day

Family Members

Witnessed by

Conclusion

"My prayer for you is that you will overflow more and more with love for others, and at the same time keep on growing in spiritual knowledge and insight, for I want you always to see clearly the difference between right and wrong, and to be inwardly clean, no one being able to criticize you from now until our Lord returns.

"May you always be doing those good, kind things which show that you are a child of God, for this will bring much praise and glory to the Lord." (Philippians 1:9-11, *The Living Bible.*)

And may the combination of your dedication to God and your commitment to your family allow you to shout to the world, "Choose ye this day whom ye will serve; . . . but as for me and my house, we will serve the Lord." (Joshua 24:15.)

References

Chapter 2

1. E. G. White, *The Ministry of Healing,* (Mt. View, CA: Pacific Press Publishing Ass., p. 372).

2. John Bowlby. *Child Care and the Growth of Love* (Baltimore, MD: Penguin Books, 1953.)

3. Robert Rosenthal and Lenore Jacobson, *Pygmalion in the Classroom* (New York: Wiley).

4. Benjamin Bloom, *Stability and Change in Human Characteristics* (New York: Wiley).

5. E. G. White, *Child Guidance,* (Mt. View, CA: Pacific Press Publishing Ass., p. 83).

6. *Ibid.,* p. 193.

7. E. G. White, *The Adventist Home,* (Mt. View, CA: Pacific Press Publishing Ass., p. 536).

8. 1 Samuel 1:8.

9. Isau Horinouchi, "Factors in Vegetarianism," *Spectrum,* vol. 5, No. 1, p.63.

10. Southeastern California Conference M. V. Department, personal communication.

11. 1 Samuel 2:26.

Chapter 9

1. Jayme Curley, et al., *The Balancing Act* (Chicago: Chicago Review Press: Swallow Press, 1976).

2. Nedra B. Belloc and Lester Breslow, "Relationship of Physical Health Status and Health Practices," *Preventive Medicine,* vol. 1, No. 3 (August, 1972), pp. 409-421.

Chapter 16

1. Based on the book, The Way Mothers Are, by Mariam Schlein. Chicago: Albert Whitman and Company, 1963.

2. Osborne, Fred, "The Relationship Between the Disposition of Hostility and Non-Self-Confirming Experiences," (Ph.D. dissertation, The Claremont Colleges, School of Theology) 1972.

WHAT IS *PARENT SCENE?*

Parent Scene is a non-profit organization providing educational materials, seminars and media presentations designed to improve parenting skills.

WHAT IS THE PURPOSE OF THE PARENT SCENE MINISTRY?

Our purpose is to provide parents with new knowledge and effective strategies for helping their children grow into mature, responsible adults. The emphasis is on encouraging children toward a healthy sense of self-worth as a way to counteract the many distressing influences of modern life.

There are simple, workable strategies that familes can use. With them, parents can set realistic goals, find new hope, revitalize placid relationships and experience renewed love and fulfillment.

These ideals are within the reach of all parents. Attaining them requires training and practice. **Parent Scene** assists parents who desire to reach these ideals.

RIGHT BEGINNING

LIVING WITH GOD'S KIDS

Dear Kay,

☐ I would like to dedicate my home and family to God's service. Please send me an 8 x 10 Home Dedication Certificate. (I have enclosed $1.00 to help with postage and handling.)

☐ Please send me a FREE copy of the Parent Scene newsletter and catalog.

☐ Please send me seminar information.

Name ______________________________

Address ______________________________

City____________________State______ZIP __________

Please send a FREE newsletter to:

Name ______________________________

Address ______________________________

City____________________State______ ZIP__________

Name ______________________________

Address ______________________________

City____________________State______ZIP __________

NAME ______________________________

Address ______________________________

City____________________State______ZIP __________